BANGKOK INSIDE OUT

DANIEL ZIV   GUY SHARETT

BANGKOK
inside out

EQUINOX
PUBLISHING
JAKARTA · SINGAPORE

EQUINOX PUBLISHING (ASIA) PTE. LTD.
PO Box 6179 JKSGN
Jakarta 12062, Indonesia

www.EquinoxPublishing.com

BANGKOK INSIDE OUT
©2005 Daniel Ziv & Guy Sharett

ISBN 979-97964-6-6

First Equinox Edition 2005

Printed in Thailand

CONTENTS

INTRODUCTION AND
RULES OF ENGAGEMENT

This book isn't really a 'guide' to Bangkok. There's no map in here or sections on where to stay and how to get around. Instead, it's a street level snapshot of a twenty-first century Southeast Asian city bursting at the seams but inching courageously forward; a snapshot of ordinary people in their urban landscape; of culture and pop culture. Our approach is raw and cheeky and irreverent at times, but we think of it as honest and real.

The Bangkok of the popular imagination is a seedy, illicit, exotic place that apparently never sleeps (or sleeps around *too much*). Most foreign-written accounts of the city play to that image or, conversely, to an ornamental version of the place as fabulously bright as the gilded stuccos of the Grand Palace, a postcard-perfect Land of Smiles.

In reality, Bangkok requires neither sexual embellishments nor imagery from its glorious past when its here-and-now is so incredibly striking. Yuppies, Chinese-Thai entrepreneurs, indie teens, civil servants, food hawkers, soap opera stars, shrewd politicians, and migrant construction workers from Isaan shape today's urban experience, not costumed traditional dancers or un-costumed Pat Pong bar girls.

And Bangkok today is a young, energetic city (most of its residents are under thirty), hardly the 'timeless' place imagined by so many glossy brochures. In *Bangkok Inside Out* we focus not on 'must see' attractions, but on the people and dynamics that make the city tick. It's no coincidence that nearly all the photos in here feature human beings rather than monuments

(we also portray two dogs and one elephant – inseparable parts of the local setting).

It is always problematic when writers comment on a place or a people not their own. No matter how much one feels a part of the scene, a foreign lens can distort impressions and, consequently, interpretations. And there is the danger of over-romanticizing the subject, or worse, being condescending.

We're hardly immune to these pitfalls, and don't claim to be 'insiders'. Much about this city still baffles us, but we've tried our best to understand Bangkok from the point of view of Bangkokians. In our research we hung out with people from all walks of life, listened to their stories and perspectives, and tried to make sense of it all.

Topics in this book are arranged alphabetically, yet some letters were so interesting they warranted more than one topic and – call us crazy – some letters received none at all. Our apologies to fans of the letters J, O, Q, V, X and Z.

Bangkok is a chaotic place, and this book probably reflects a bit of that madness. But lately it's also a city that's constantly bettering itself. It's bouncing back from recession, basic services have improved, and it's becoming an increasingly cosmopolitan place – full of enthusiasm and creative energy. So for all the quips, satires and dirt we dish out on these pages, we hope our love for this amazing city still shines through.

Daniel Ziv & Guy Sharett
Bangkok, November 2004
bio@equinoxpublishing.com

11

In loving memory of
Shlomo Sharett,
passionate tug boat skipper
and intrepid traveler

AMULETS

เครื่องราง

Bangkok's Pra Chan sidewalk amulet market is a great place to witness Buddhist Thailand's vibrant subtext of animist superstition, omens and magical power. Vendors and customers alike hunch over precious Buddhist amulets with obvious passion, painstaking concentration and a persistent fussiness.

Amulets are thought to heal, protect, boost sexual charm or bring good fortune, and nearly every Thai carries at least one such *phra khrueng* or wears one as a pendant. Blessed by noted Thai monks, the talismans are usually an encased clay or metal image of Buddha, King Rama V or a revered holy figure. Politicians have been known to give them to Thais embarking on potentially dangerous overseas missions – peacekeepers to East Timor, even farm hands bound for Israel.

Despite transactions estimated at $250,000 per day in Bangkok alone, the words 'buy' and 'sell' are not officially applicable to the amulet trade. Treating holy items as property is forbidden. Instead, collectors formally 'rent' these talismans from shops, temples or streetside traders. Most Thais acquire amulets for their spiritual value intending to keep them within the family forever, passing them down through the generations. Amulets are sacred symbols and so must never be placed, for instance, in one's pocket or in the vicinity of one's feet.

An amulet's value depends on which monastery made it, which monk blessed it, in whose image it is cast, its perceived track record of bringing luck or protection to its owner, its rarity or antiquity and – to a somewhat lesser extent – its beauty. Some images are recast over certain periods; an original might be five hundred years old, whereas its remodeled version might be just fifty.

When the industry peaked in the mid-1990s, about forty different magazines in Thailand were devoted to amulet collecting and an estimated one million Thais collected amulets either for personal use or investment. The amulet trade took a hit in the late 1990s when the region's devastating financial crisis drove many Thais to pawn beloved talismans for badly needed cash. And Thailand's revered monkhood was tainted by a series of scandals – think embezzlement, booze and women – that shocked the public and diminished the value of certain amulets. With the country's economy bouncing back in recent years and monks generally steering clear of scandal, the amulet world is enjoying a revival.

Fans of beauty pageants should make Bangkok their permanent home. In fact anyone who has ever dreamed of entering such a contest is certain to find his or her specialty category here. Switch on local TV anytime and you're nearly guaranteed to catch yet another beauty contest. "What is *this* one?!" you protest to your Bangkokian friends, "Miss Thailand was just a few months ago!" until they patiently explain that "This one is strictly for ladyboys from Northeast Thailand, who haven't had the operation yet…."

In addition to the conventional Miss Thailand, Miss Thailand World and Miss Thailand Universe, enter Jumbo Queen Pageant, an annual contest for extra-large gals, also intended as an ode to Thailand's diminishing number of wild elephants (see "Urban Elephants"); Miss AC/DC – a contest for ladyboys in which contestants are supposedly judged for intelligence rather than beauty, and dress in tacky national costumes from around the world; and Miss Khanthong (literally 'Miss Old Maid'), in which participants must be over thirty and single, possess at least a bachelor's degree and a 'good job'. Recent contestants included ladies with PhDs, a former national team volleyball player and an ex-TV star. Although women's NGOs protested the contest because it "made fun of old maids," it was a huge success and other Asian countries lined up to buy the rights to hold similar contests.

For years these contests have provided a stage for poor country girls – or ladyboys – hoping to make it big in the City of Angels. Candidates are typically trained by a full time beauty pageant guru, who teaches the pretty young hopefuls how to walk, talk and giggle ("Put your hand over your mouth…good, fingers must be at a twenty-degree angle to your mouth, now giggle…Yes!").

Audiences at these contests consist mostly of men, many of whom come armed with binoculars for a closer view. In 2003, days after the Miss Thailand World beauty pageant, Thai tabloids stunned readers with photos from the wedding ceremony of supposedly single Jatuporn "Joy" Saengthong, the second runner-up. All candidates must declare they are single to qualify. "I didn't mean to deceive anyone. I was only chasing my dream, like other girls. I was hoping it could happen to me, just like Cinderella," said a tearful Khun Joy.

BUSES

รถเมล์

Buses in Bangkok epitomize the city's diversity. As with accommodation, food and sex, the options are numerous and confusing: little green buses at B3.5 (around 10 cents) per ride; red and white buses with battered wooden floors; blue and white ones with hanging fans; big air-con buses with comfy seats; swankier 'microbuses' for B20 (50 cents) a ride; and modern orange buses whose conductors greet boarding passengers with a soft "*sawatdii kha.*"

The Bangkok Bus Experience begins at the bus stop. Passengers usually opt not to wait there at all (boring!) and instead stand thirty meters before it. They fear the driver might somehow fail to notice their frantic jumping and waving and shoot right on by. Then comes boarding. Buses don't actually come to a full stop, but glide towards passenger-hopefuls so that some may have a slim chance of actually hopping on. Once they do, the conductor – normally a woman with a voice shrill enough to rival Frau Farbissina of Austin Powers fame – shouts "*Pai!*" ("Go!") at the driver, who dutifully stomps on the accelerator with all his fatalistic might.

'Frau' then approaches newly boarded passengers with her *krabok* – a heavy cylinder-shaped metal case with coins and paper ticket rolls. Bank notes are folded fan-like between her thick, sturdy fingers, allowing her to dish out change even during harrowing jolts and turns. Frau shakes her *krabok* loudly when pacing down the aisle, so no one can ignore her and avoid paying the fare.

Upon receiving fares, Frau tears tickets along the edge of the *krabok* in a quick, one-handed, pirouetted movement. This is Bangkok performance art par excellence. Frau completes the act by handing passengers their tickets and change, pressing her finger into their palm to ensure the ticket won't fall out. Then she'll sit on the hot engine cover next to the driver and chat him up until the next stop. Like male drivers pretty much everywhere, Bangkok bus drivers are obsessed with one thing: passing through traffic junctions before the light turns red. This is why they sometimes ignore frantically jumping and waving commuters at bus stops (see above).

For all the chaos inside this speeding, vibrating wreck, passengers manage to remain composed and *suphaap* ('polite'). People gladly offer their seats to mothers and toddlers, and seated passengers will hold the books and bags of people standing beside them. On the other hand – according to one recent survey – nearly 25% of female passengers have experienced sexual harassment, like men "looking at them strangely," standing uncomfortably close or even groping their breasts.

CHAO ISAAN

ชาวอีสาน

For most of the year, villages in Isaan – Thailand's northeastern, poorest region – are inhabited by elderly people, young children and a handful of women taking care of them. The other *Chao Isaan* ('Isaan people') can be found in Bangkok: Most of the city's taxi and *motosai* drivers, construction workers, waiters, cooks, maids and sex workers come from Isaan. Nearly all of them work long, hard hours and send savings back to the village to support parents or cover school fees for their kids.

Behind the scenes and beneath the city's glamorous surface, *Chao Isaan* are the powerful engine that makes Bangkok roar. During the rice-planting season from May to July, many of them return to the village to help family in the fields, and Bangkok is virtually crippled without its trusty service professionals.

Although many Bangkokians look down on *Chao Isaan* as unsophisticated villagers with odd cultural traits, nearly everybody speaks at least a few words of the Isaan language. *Luuk thuung* and *morlam*, northeastern musical styles, are big on national TV. And Isaan cuisine's gift to the world, the *som tam* papaya salad, has become a flagship dish of Thai cuisine.

We encountered two friendly Isaan sisters working and living together at one of Bangkok's countless construction sites. Their small cluster of friends and relatives seemed cut-and-pasted straight out of their home village into the harsh Bangkok environment.

The sisters earn just B160 ($4) per day and live in a tiny plywood-and-metal shack. A rare day off is spent visiting relatives who work in factories or at other construction sites. Nails in the foot are the most common injury here, but the occasional drunk fellow workman will tumble straight off a building. After work, the sisters watch soap operas and *luuk thuung* music programs on a small TV bought with their savings. Their favorite reading material: soap opera synopses. They spend around B50 ($1.25) on food each day, and call their children in the village nearly every evening on their mobile phone.

One of the sisters, Lung, says it's common to see people in their migrant community crying at night, missing their kids and homes. Indeed, a favorite phrase in Isaan folk songs is *kit teung baan* ('to miss home') – like a giant pall of yearning rising out from taxis, food stalls, hotels and brothels, looming above this alien city before drifting slowly toward the Northeast.

CHATUCHAK

จตุจักร

Our friend René, a Mexican animator and long-term Bangkok dilettante, compares the city's Chatuchak Market to the Hogwarts School of Harry Potter lore: When you move around it everything starts to shift and by the time you return to where you began, it is no longer the same. René hardly ever makes sense, but we suspect his point in this case is that if you see something you like in Chatuchak, buy it right away because you'll probably never find it again. After enough sweltering hours of browsing on a recent visit, it seemed like even the sky train station was no longer where we last left it.

Orientation probably won't get any easier as Southeast Asia's largest market seems intent on ballooning by the month. At last count its estimated 15,000 stalls covered an area of 120,000 square meters. Each weekend over 300,000 visitors descend on the place, combining to spend upwards of $800,000. The bird trade alone boggles the mind (and damages the ears): Around 36,000 winged things are sold at Chatuchak each day, including endangered species. Indeed, the raucous pet section with its tarantulas, snakes, iguanas and droopy-eyed, please-take-me-home-with-you puppies must be seen to be believed. Even carnivorous piranhas are sold here illegally for B3,000 (about $72) a pop.

But Chatuchak (also nicknamed JJs – from the alternative spelling, *Jatujak*) is more than just a bustling, ever-expanding market. In recent years it has become a hip scene in its own right. Outdoor pubs offering ice-cold draught beer and modish cafés serving hearty Thai fare are nestled between stalls hawking 70s retro fashion, vintage Levi's Red Tab and Big E jeans, designer incense sticks and battered Japanese army fatigues. Even ultra-trendy Princess Ubolrat has been spotted scouring for fashionable threads here, further adding a notch to Chatuchak's 'cool' factor.

In fact we can hardly think of anything wrong with a place that offers easy access, great food, a trendy atmosphere, excellent bargains, a kaleidoscope of sights and sounds, and a choice of virtually every product under the sun. Perhaps that last point hints at the only real downside: Chatuchak can get mighty hot around midday, so get there early to beat the heat and crowds.

CHIC

'Chic' is difficult to define, because it's more a mood, aesthetic sense or interpretation than anything tangible ("But what do we actually *mean* by 'chic'?!", Guy would pester Daniel over a stale breakfast at a seaside Hua Hin café). Suffice it to say that in Bangkok, modern day chic is but a long lost cousin of the ancient Thai aesthetic instinct. These two forces blend beautifully (when they're not clashing wildly) in bars, shops and restaurants, and on billboards and video screens all over the city. Chic also means that if ten years ago you could get a perfectly nice pair of chopsticks for B10 on Charoen Krung Road, today you'll shell out B350 for the same pair – wrapped in silk and packaged in recycled paper – at a boutique in Siam Discovery Center.

Wealthy, foreign-educated young Thais are behind this unstoppable wave of self-consciously trendy minimalism. They return home overflowing with inspiration from swanky Manhattan bars, posh design schools in London and the many issues of *Wallpaper* magazine that line the translucent shelves of their Lang Suan studio lofts. Thankfully, daddy usually has enough cash to spare so that young Khun Oak can realize his dream of opening Southeast Asia's first Scandinavian-themed glass noodle bar or a neon-lit Silom café serving eight-dollar energy smoothies to the relaxing sounds of Buddha Bar VII. It's a fine line that separates fusion from confusion.

There is, of course, an undeniable link between Bangkok's vibrant gay community (see "Gay") and the current design revolution. Some of the most stylish hangouts, like the cozier joints along Silom Road, are popular gay meeting spots.

The Bed Supper Club (pictured here) is certainly more Matrix than Mae Hong Son, but many of Bangkok's new outposts of chic aren't nearly so otherworldly, and do a great service by offering fresh new interpretations of local aesthetic tradition. China Journal tea house in Thong Lor or the cafés along Phra Athit Road (see "Phra Athit") are charming examples of young, tasteful innovation.

When we want the experience of traveling to a foreign place but don't have time or money, we'll usually hop a river taxi to the district of Yaowarat, Bangkok's Chinatown. Here, in an ornate cultural bubble, a distinctive, almost magical atmosphere prevails: The aromas and flavors are unique, the fruits are strange and always succulent, and in the early evening along Yaowarat Road, even the light feels different.

Stores stacked floor to ceiling with pungent herbal medicines share shophouse rows with restaurants showcasing precious shark's fin delicacies. The smells of freshly-roasted chestnuts and grilled seafood from corner food stalls compete with the stench of fish from a wet market around the corner and the delicate fragrance of incense wafting out from nearby temples. Gem traders, gold dealers and household appliance vendors labor beneath a chaotic jungle of signs that at night turn Yaowarat into a neon-splashed mini-Hong Kong, with all the friendliness of Thailand.

But Yaowarat is merely the hub. Chinese culture permeates nearly every aspect of life in Bangkok, from architecture and cuisine to business and spirituality, so much so that the entire capital often feels like a Chinese city superimposed on a Thai landscape.

Ever since their arrival in the nineteenth century, Chinese immigrants were deeply involved in shaping the city's economy and culture. All the while, Thai-Chinese intermarriage was so common that Bangkok's demography today is an ethnic muddle in which most Bangkokians can trace a fair bit of Chinese blood in them. Thailand's Prime Minister Thaksin Shinawatra for instance, is of Sino-Thai lineage as are many members of his cabinet.

In fact, Chinese Thais are not really regarded as a minority, and Bangkok is mercifully free of the racial preoccupations and tensions that characterize neighboring capitals like Jakarta and Kuala Lumpur. So complete was the Chinese assimilation and influence here, suggests William Warren in his authoritative book on the city, that "as far as Bangkok is concerned, the result has been the steady decline, virtually the disappearance, of anything purely Thai."

31

COMICS

การ์ตูน

On a bus or the sky train, or while waiting for a friend at the mall, young Bangkokians frequently pull a comic book from their bag, bury their head inside it, and break into a wide, sustained grin. Who ever said Thai teens don't read?!

Since few comic aficionados will invest B35 (about $1) in a 'book' that's devoured in under an hour, comic libraries, usually situated near universities and high schools, are insanely popular. Membership is as simple as paying B50 ($1.25) a year and handing over your ID card. You can then borrow a colorful 180-page volume for about B4 per day.

Hard-core fans head for secondhand or discount shops in Chatuchak and MBK, which offer a wide selection and low prices. Some hobbyists become addicted: A salesman at a Siam Square shop recalled one Bangkok student who bought books totaling B10,000 (around $240) as an annual supply before leaving to study at an American university. Nobody seems to know how she did in her studies.

Comics are usually imported from Japan and sold 'as is', with only the text bubbles translated into Thai and the page direction reversed. Much of this material has become an inseparable part of local pop culture: Practically every Bangkokian is familiar, for instance, with Doraemon, the earless, cat-like robot. Most of these comic books deal with the quest for self-fulfillment through martial arts training, sports or saving the world. Girlie, romantic versions are called *ta wan* ('sweet eyes' – like those of their heroines).

Predictably, the fad is spun for all it's worth: comic-themed collectibles like T-shirts and stationery line the shelves of department stores across the city; a column in the *Matichon* weekly magazine offers psychoanalysis of comic characters by a practicing psychiatrist; and one local publisher hopes to reach a wider market through comic books based on classical Thai literature.

One original Thai creation is *Taleung* ('cheeky'), a series peppered with sexual innuendos and puns in succinct Bangkokian lingo. The authors took unusual poetic license with the spelling so as to mimic the spoken language. We won't comment on the size of women's breasts in these books (OK – they are *huge*), but they speak volumes about men and wishful thinking. That's alright though: In frenetic Bangkok, comics serve as magic capsules that whisk people from a hot bus ride in a huge traffic jam to a world where anything is possible.

Conceptually, do-it-yourself dining joints seem like a dumb idea. One normally goes to restaurants to get *out* of the kitchen and relax, not pay good money to sit around a table, cook one's own food and still get screamed at by Auntie Jaeng for letting her tiger prawn go Cajun by forgetting to flip it in time.

Yet such is the popularity of DIY dining in Bangkok, especially among raucous groups of students, that any self-respecting shopping mall will have at least one of the four big chains – MK, Coca Suki, Daidomon or BBQ Plaza. Many malls host all four.

The Suki restaurants offer Japanese-inspired Sukiyaki: raw ingredients ordered off a menu and dumped into a big pot of boiling water in the center of the table, to be stirred by, added to and served from by the customers themselves. Raw ingredients include seafood, meat, vegetables, wontons, eggs, and other fresh delights. The Daidomon version places a sunken grill in the table center, and has diners huddling through the smoke to flip meat, bask in the aroma, and maybe even manage a conversation.

For all the concentration and hard work required, DIY dining has its advantages: First, these places offer great value-for-money, some even staging all-you-can-grill lunch and dinner deals. Second, in a relatively non-confrontational, collective society, this sort of communal cooking sidesteps the need to argue about where to dine or what to order. Third, it offers all the fun of cooking (and Thais love to cook) without having to clean up the mess. And fourth, in the absence of any sort of substantive conversation topic, this dining style provides a whole array of logistics to fuss over and keep everyone engaged ("Nong Kwan, don't you drop those in! You know grandma can't eat pork balls or morning glory!"). Similarly, someone losing a perfectly good piece of sirloin into the coals because of inferior chopstick skills can spark a huge family squabble. DIY dining halls are not quiet places.

35

Durian is the Southeast Asian 'King of Fruit' nobody can ignore. In Singapore it is banned in public places due to its overpowering odor; in Bangkok it is sometimes said to symbolize the city – large, spiky and smelly on the surface, soft and tasty on the inside. Its popularity here is such that for a long while durian-flavored condoms were sold at the counter of every neighborhood 7-Eleven.

Foreign travel writers and horticulturists have described it rather uncharitably as "French custard passed through a sewer pipe" and "rotten onions with Limburger cheese and low-tide seaweed."

But markets and supermarkets across Bangkok carry the unmistakable durian scent. The city's donut shops are more likely to stock Durian Cream than Chocolate Glaze and traditional Thai sweets and chips are made from durian pulp or extract. A popular local delicacy is durian in coconut milk sauce on sticky rice. Yum.

Small durian candy factories dot the countryside in eastern Thailand where some of the best durian is grown. Workers there must endure the fruit's smell, and most – particularly Northeasterners – last just a few weeks before moving on to more fragrant employment.

Such is the love here for durian that enthusiasts debate the fruit's attributes in internet chat groups and religiously attend annual durian fairs. Websites devoted to the fruit border on the obsessive, presenting durian photos and 'field reports' with all the graphic flair and bravado of a well-crafted porn site ("Rare Durians of Borneo!" was the title of one particularly racy link). Indeed, the fruit is thought by some to stimulate the libido. According to a Malay proverb, "When the durian falls down, the sarongs rise up." And Thais like to caution against eating durian while drinking beer, for fear that one's stomach will explode.

Durian is native to Sumatra and Borneo and the word *duri* means 'thorn' in Malay, but Thailand has become the leading player and exporter. Thai growers produce an estimated one million tons of the fruit each year, mainly out of Chanthaburi, Rayong and Nonthaburi provinces. Of Southeast Asia's three hundred-odd varieties, Thailand's legendary Monthong ('Golden Pillow') is arguably the region's most popular. No wonder each time Philippine President and hard-core durian fan Gloria Macapagal Arroyo visits Thailand, her hosts prepare a durian buffet that includes durian ice cream and other culinary concoctions that are clearly in breach of the Geneva Convention.

Bangkok may be renowned for its sacred Buddhist temples, but if there is one truly sanctified place for Bangkok's high society (see "Hi-So/Lo-So"), it is the Emporium shopping center, a gleaming upmarket shrine to conspicuous consumption.

Only here can one encounter that endearing mélange of bored Japanese housewives, wailing toddlers in tow, eagerly inspecting ten-thousand-dollar Cartier bracelets; bar girls embarking on a new adventure with a fresh-off-the-plane male victim; trendy businessmen huddled in a rebranding meeting sucking furiously on overpriced lattes; Bangkok society ladies with ten-kilo hairdos filing in and out of designer boutiques; and five gay soulmates from Hong Kong on a deliciously wild shopping expedition. Yes, on an average day all of these characters and many more, can be seen gliding along Emporium's shiny marble floors like so many Captain Stubings on the Aloha Deck.

As for the merchandise on offer, there is little tolerance for counterfeit goods (see "Fakes") at this prestigious Bangkok bazaar. The Guccis and Pradas here – like the price tags on their bags, shoes and pashmina scarves – are all painfully genuine.

So popular is this mall amongst Bangkok brats that it has produced a sub-culture all its own, personified by what we call the Bangkok Emporium Girl (BEG). She was born to a Swiss father and a Thai mother (see "Luuk Kreung") and grew up in Basle, which explains why she does not speak a word of Thai. Money was never a problem and therefore a BEG considers B450 (around $11) a perfectly fair price for papaya salad. Typical BEGs are slim, desperately shallow and are "doing a bit of modeling" before deciding on their "path in life". They'll enter the Emporium Mother Ship for a facial, a film and an icy Frappuccino before moving on to one of Bangkok's ultra-stylish fitness gyms, all the while reporting in real time to friends via mobile phone about these exciting activities.

For many working class Thais, Emporium is the presentable face of Bangkok when accompanying a foreign friend around town. Ironically, there is almost nothing Thai in a space filled wall-to-wall with Bvlgari, Bang & Oulfsen and Boots. But arguing with perceptions is futile: 'Sunday Jazz' here usually means hits by The Carpenters, Abba and Bee Gees, followed by a pet show in the atrium. And this is the beauty of it all.

FAKES

ของปลอม

Although the Thai government has been fighting counterfeit goods for years, Bangkok's streets remain inundated with fake merchandise. This exciting city offers not just the conventional selection of knock-off Polo shirts, movie DVDs, and Yves Saint Laurent briefcases, but also fake gemstones, imitation antiques and an impressive array of fraudulent documents.

Novices seeking the occasional travel discount pick up international student cards at stalls along Khaosan Road. If your mother harbored dreams that you'd become a musicology apprentice at the Hochschule für Music und Darstellende Kunst in Vienna, this might be the chance to put a smile on her face after everything she's been through with you. Forged EFL teaching certificates and even full university degrees are sold here, too – convenient for backpackers aspiring to teach English in Thailand when they are not can really speak it so good.

Hard-core counterfeit connoisseurs can score a genuine passport and travel incognito to Rio. In 2004, Thai and Spanish police uncovered a large Bangkok-based ring that forged passports and sold them to drug traffickers and other criminals. In one ring leader's home, police found dozens of perfectly forged French, Belgian, Spanish and Kiwi passports selling for $1,800 a piece.

At evening souvenir stalls along Silom, Patpong and Sukhumvit roads, it is hard to find merchandise that is *not* a knock-off. Most impressive are the wristwatch dealers, who offer fake timepieces in three quality tiers: Rolex watches come in a $30 model (cheap-looking, hardly functions), a $75 version (not bad, but unconvincing upon close inspection) and a $300 rendition, fine enough to impress any rich snob on your company's board of directors.

Computer software piracy has reached epidemic proportions in Thailand. A recent report claims the country is home to at least one hundred optical media plants operating illicitly with a combined production capacity of up to one billion discs per year for the international market. Another study estimated that as much as 98% of entertainment software in Thailand is pirated.

In Bangkok, any socially inept sixteen-year-old techno geek knows Panthip Plaza, the city's candy store of bootlegged software. Police frequently raid the shopping arcade to little avail, since distributors and vendors enjoy protection from patrons in high up places – usually senior police officers, politicians or army generals.

40

FARANG

The term loosely translates as 'white foreigner,' and depending on the context can range from an innocent description to an outright slur. Either way, any westerner hanging out in Bangkok for more than a few hours is certain to hear the word uttered around them. The expression is so broad it can relate to a French CEO, a Khaosan Road hippie, an Australian NGO worker, or just about anything that is white and moves. Actually, scruffy Khaosan Road backpackers earned their very own, rather more elaborate, term: *farang khii nok* ('birdshit whitey'), which suggests that Thai society is able to distinguish between the many exciting nuances of our white human state.

Farang demarcates the cultural border between Thai society and foreigners, mirroring their different ways of seeing the world. As 'Bangkok Phil' points out on his outspoken website (www.bangkokmouth.com), most Thais will never understand why *farang* wear shorts away from the beach, kiss and hug old friends, or how they manage to drink beer without ice. They are also puzzled that we'd ever choose to walk somewhere when we can easily take a *motosai* or taxi.

After a while in Bangkok, we found ourselves instinctively using the F-word in reference to other foreigners or even ourselves (schizophrenia is a drag). Sometimes, when we're on a non-air-con bus surrounded exclusively by Thai passengers and feeling terribly special, another foreigner steps on board and violates our exotic territory. This is when we sneer at him with contempt and mumble *"farang"* under our breath.

Some *farang* have made their way into the Bangkok ethos, like Jim Thompson, an American credited with pioneering the Thai silk weaving industry; Nancy Chandler, who created the popular city map that bears her name; Australian Andrew Biggs, a famous Bangkok journalist and television host; and Jonas Anderson, a Swede who grew up in Thailand and became one of the country's most popular crooners of *Luuk Thung* (northeastern Thai music). Thais love foreigners who master their language and adopt their way of life, so when they see young, blonde Jonas wearing a flower garland on his collar and belting out Isaan-language tunes, they simply melt.

Most foreigners don't go to such lengths. Some find the language too tricky or cannot find the time to study and end up living in an expatriate bubble. They're unable to read a Thai newspaper or understand local TV and radio, and unless they've got a Thai partner, tend to have few local friends. Alas, even those who do speak Thai cannot change the color of their skin, and will remain *farang* outsiders forever.

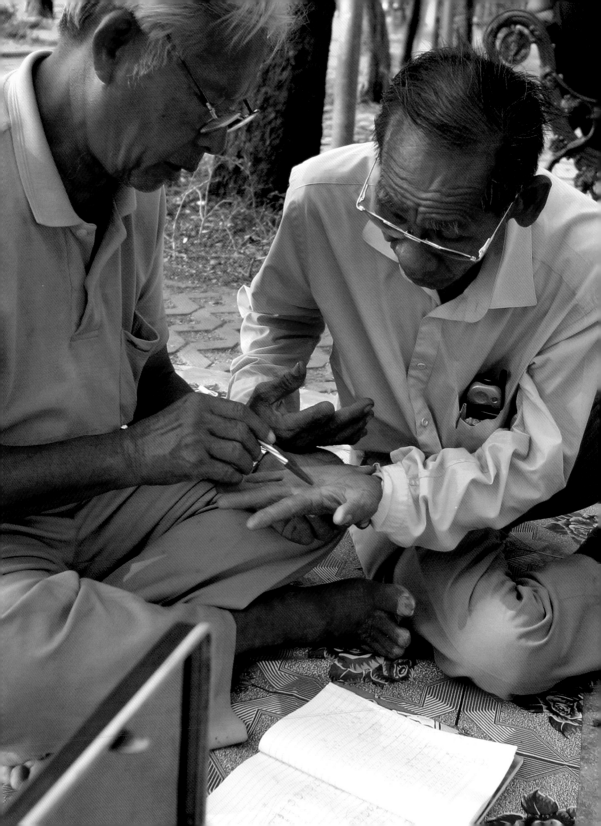

If fortune telling is any sort of barometer, Bangkok must be the quintessential City of the Future. Stroll along Ratchadamnern Avenue and you'll find the International Astrological Association, the Astrological Association of Thailand and the Thailand Astrological Foundation. Between them, over thirty courses are offered for all manner of fortune telling, from Chinese astrology to tarot card reading and even birthmark interpretation ('Mole Analysis 101', anybody?)

Many students attend these quasi-synonymous establishments to become *mor-doo* (literally 'doctor that can see') or *hoan* (astrologers) for the money: If you're really good you can bag B1,000 (about $25) an hour. A more common rate, though, is about B100-200. Some students are MA and PhD graduates simply looking to earn extra baht; and no, you don't need special skills to be admitted to astrology school. Although it all sounds quite easy, older, experienced *mor-doo* with a proven record of accuracy are considered most reliable and command the highest fees.

While nearly every neighborhood has its local *mor-doo*, a favorite hangout for Bangkok clairvoyants is the north end of the Sanam Luang royal park. Here there's usually one psychic for every three tamarind trees, seated on a plastic tarp and armed with requisite props: a cardboard sign advertising their service; a briefcase packed with photos of monks or Hindu gods; a magnifying glass for palm reading; a pile of paper and manual for calculating a client's birth date; and a chart listing possible positions of birthmarks and moles and their interpretation. Their usual sales tactic? Beckoning to passersby by calling out "You are clouded by bad luck!" Most people are too superstitious to resist.

Thais are also huge fans of horoscopes, fed straight into the vein through every possible media: newspapers, radio, TV, internet, and SMS. In fact, serious magazines sometimes differentiate themselves from lesser publications by *not* including a horoscope page.

Traditionally, most fortune-telling clients were women, but with the recent rise of Bangkok's metrosexual male, more men are seeking psychic help (giving Bangkok's *mor-doo* – brace for the pun – mor to doo!). Favorite consultation topics are love, children (especially for choosing names), career prospects and financial woes.

Although gambling is illegal in Thailand (other than the state lottery, kickboxing matches and horse races), underground gambling is everywhere. In Bangkok, according to one survey, nearly a third of the population places unauthorized bets quite regularly, and each month Bangkokians collectively manage to gamble away some B8 billion (around $195 million).

Local betting during the three-week Euro 2004 football championship was estimated at B33 billion ($810 million). The number of robberies in Bangkok rose sharply during the tournament, and according to police reports many suspects cited heavy gambling debts as the motive. Some ten thousand other gamblers found a better solution: hours before the opening game they hopped across the border to the Cambodian town of Poipet, where five casinos offered bona fide football betting. Backstreet cockfights and stadium kickboxing are other favorite ways for working-class Bangkokians to lose their hard-earned money.

The maximum penalty for illegal gambling is a year in prison, but police must first catch gamblers red-handed. Bangkok police try to raid illegal gambling dens, but owners often get tipped off by corrupt policemen. This is what happened one Sunday afternoon in 2002 when three hundred policemen tried to storm the building of Madame Jeh Pao, a well-known industry figure in Eastern Bangkok. For thirty long minutes neighbors prevented police from entering the building. When police finally broke in they found forty people, some hiding in the toilets and under tables. Since no one was actually caught gambling, police could make no arrests. Jeh Pao expressed outrage at the disturbance, telling newspapers she was merely hosting a few dozen of her closest friends for afternoon tea and didn't understand what all the fuss was about.

Gambling in Bangkok is hardly a sporadic phenomenon and is prevalent at all levels of society – in schools, at offices and on the street. Bookies busily collect bets in an underground industry that promises far bigger returns than the state lottery (see "Lottery"). In recent years the Thai government has made noises about possibly legalizing casino gambling, sparking heated public debate on the issue.

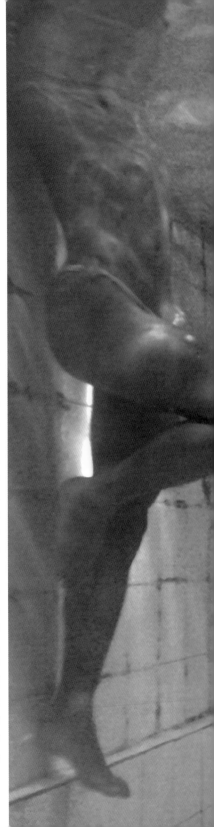

GAY

เกย์

Men who enjoy men flock from all corners of the earth to the pink City of Angels, where they can embrace a gay lifestyle far from the watchful gaze of parents, friends and sometimes even wives and children.

So vast and vibrant is Bangkok's gay society (no numbers available, for obvious reasons) that Chuwit Kamolvisit, a decidedly straight massage parlor tycoon and candidate for city governor, promised to develop "a homosexual zone à la Greenwich Village" should he win the election (he lost). Gay organizations promised him their vote if he allowed them to visit schools and teach gay students how to behave in society, "so that they don't marry women and end up getting divorced." While Thai society generally accepts homosexuality, many gays are nevertheless expected to follow cultural conventions and produce grandchildren for their anxious parents.

Bangkok's epicenter of gay entertainment is a cluster of alleys (*soi*) lined with bars, saunas, chic cafés and nightclubs just off Silom Road. One establishment even features an erotic mermaid show ('mer*man*' in Zoolanderspeak) with guys in bikini bottoms – and eventually without bikini bottoms – aquadancing in a huge aquarium to the crowd's obvious delight. If you thought the whales at Sea World did neat tricks, wait till you see the Shamus here.

In a worrying development for Bangkok's proud crowd, Silom Soi 4, previously the exclusive domain of gay establishments, was recently hijacked by straight folk. Someone understood that a promiscuous environment, stylish bars and great music might appeal to a wider market. New bohemian clubs suddenly mushroomed, confusing indigenous gays who until then had never needed to activate their gaydars.

Gay culture prospers in Bangkok, with an openly gay film and art scene, annual gay and lesbian festivals and little, if any, discrimination in the job market. But it's hardly Amsterdam or San Francisco. Gays rarely walk hand in hand outside the Silom enclave, and Thai parents don't exactly jump for joy when their son finally explains why he's not particularly interested in the gorgeous girl next door – even if her father *does* own the Toyota franchise for Thailand. The Ministry of Culture recently asked that TV stations reduce the number of gay characters in their shows, particularly transvestites (see "Kathoey") so as "not to encourage children to become homosexual."

If this city is a real-life movie set, surely its ubiquitous mobile vendors are the colorful extras that provide texture, sound and smell to the chaotic daily drama that is Bangkok.

Hawkers push, drag or carry carts around town, flogging just about everything under the hot Bangkok sun: noodles, plants, filter coffee, fruit, car air freshener, pastries, ice cream or floor mops. They'll sometimes set themselves apart through a particular horn, ring or holler. Each has a regular route and they'll normally park their carts for short periods of time in selected locations.

A few years ago the Bangkok Metropolitan Office decided to instill method into the madness and required all street vendors to register for permits to trade on city sidewalks. Annual permits cost B500 (about $12.50). Over 44,000 hawkers registered but an estimated 15,000 traders continued working clandestinely. Hawkers caught operating outside their designated stretch of pavement face a B2,000 fine. The hidden costs, however, don't appear in the municipality's account books: Nearly all vendors pay protection fees to extortion rackets who lay claim to the different vending zones. "I need to be very cautious where I wander with my cart so that I don't step into anyone else's area," explained our neighborhood fry queen while obsessively scrubbing down her wok.

If sticking to one's turf wasn't already a pain in the butt, the rise of hypermarkets is eating into small vendor profits everywhere. Our favorite bra seller at Phra Khanong market has made a career out of vilifying a certain supermarket chain she claims slashes its bra prices "like there is no tomorrow" ("*meuan mai mii phrung nii*"). Not all vendors are so desperate, however: One food hawker in Thonburi admitted to raking in profits of up to B2,000 (around $50) per day.

Finally, an anthropological tip, free of charge: When buying from a stall, Bangkokians tend to walk straight up to the vendor and announce what they want the moment they arrive on the scene, only then moving into a proper queue. Many uninitiated *farang* misinterpret this as jumping the line, but it's not. We hope this somehow contributes to a greater sense of love, understanding and tolerance around town.

53

Bangkok *Hi-So* (High Society) folks are a unique breed, utterly detached from what most people consider real life, yet they are the movers and shakers of this country. They are usually the bosses of *Lo-So* (Low Society) types, and are often – though not always – of Chinese descent. *Hi-So* folks have a slew of people taking care of them: Illegal Burmese maids look after their gargantuan homes, Isaan drivers shuttle them around town, gardeners tend to their vast grounds, while nannies are at their children's beck and call.

Whisked smoothly from one air-conditioned bubble to the next, *Hi-So* types hardly ever breathe the city's polluted air, viewing Bangkok through tinted glass as if the outside world were a movie about someone else's life.

Some *Hi-So* we know have never boarded a public bus in their life, taken a boat along a *khlong*, nor the sky train or subway. Most speak flawless English, the product of years at boarding schools and universities abroad.

On the following pages we present indispensable guides for shocking and impressing your *Hi-So* Bangkokian friends. You might want to practice these first on your hamster or little brother. In any case, we cannot accept responsibility for the consequences. 55

How to Shock *Hi-So* Bangkokian Friends

- Urge them to take the boat along Khlong Saen Saeb from Siam to Bang Kapi, "because it's so much cheaper than a taxi."

- Confiscate their mobile phone, then answer all calls in Danish, explaining "Khun Noi er flyttet til en lille landsby tæt ved Trat for at hjælpe sin familie på kokosnøds-plantagen" ("Khun Noi has moved to a small village near Trat to help out on the family coconut plantation.")

- Invite five *Hi-So* friends to a dinner at a posh restaurant. Upon arrival, insist on noodles at the roadside stall outside "because it's more authentic." Then claim the noodles are *mai aroi* ('not delicious') and inform everyone it's time to go back into the restaurant.

- *Wai* (join palms together in a traditional greeting gesture) every single person you see in the street, even those younger than you. *Wai* even kids and soi dogs.

- Bring four shabby Khaosan backpacker friends to a formal reception at a five star Bangkok hotel and insist on introducing them to everyone, including the Minister of Transportation and his wife.

- Claim your mother is a macramé teacher from Surat Thani and your father is a ladyboy from Croatia who met on a Nakhon Ratchasima military base thirty years ago. Use your hands to demonstrate the size of your dad's boobs at the time.

- When you rendezvous with friends at a coffee shop, invite your *motosai* driver into the café and announce: "Everybody, meet my driver, James."

- Haggle aggressively for a discount from the little boy selling flower garlands in the street and claim aloud that "These people make thousands of baht a month, I've seen a documentary about it."

How to Impress *Hi-So* Bangkokian friends

- Moan repeatedly about your servant, who recently vanished with the gardener's cousin – after all you've done for her!

- Make sure everybody knows you never ride the sky train "because I feel it violates my personal freedom."

- Sneer about a friend who just had a facial at MBK, and say, "Never been. I usually go to The Regent."

- Whine that you are hungry and explain that you haven't eaten since early morning because the servants returned to their village for New Years and you can't remember where the kitchen is.

- Insert English words in every Thai phrase, for impact. From time to time ask: "How do you say that in Thai? Ouch, I keep forgetting words!"

- Even better: Speak Thai in an American accent (especially the letter 'r') although you've never been to the U.S.

- In conversations, insert anecdotes such as: "And then, at 3 a.m. in Rome, we decided we just *had* to eat fried rice. Luckily I know the Thai chef at the Savoy, so we woke him up. You should have seen poor Khun Suthiphong frying rice for us in his pajamas!"

- Have lots of fancy teddy bears in your car, with aristocratic names like Arthur, Leopold and Henrietta.

- Tell your friends how you stood confused in the parking lot for nearly ten minutes yesterday because you couldn't remember which car you brought. Giggle with mock embarrassment and say: "I guess that's what happens when you've got too many cars."

- Mention nonchalantly how your dog, André, was just offered a role in a Channel Three soap opera, "but is still weighing his options."

INDIE MUSIC

เพลงอินดี้

Melodies seem to run through the veins of most Bangkokians. Whether they're crooning karaoke tunes, singing along to live acoustic guitar ballads at a café, screaming to Thongchai 'Bird' McIntyre pop tunes at a packed stadium concert, or taking in some jazz at the ever-popular *Saxophone* or *Brown Sugar* clubs, the city's younger generation lives and breathes music. Even HM King Bhumiphol Adulyadej has managed a shadow career as an accomplished composer and talented saxophonist.

Just beneath the surface of this mainstream music world rages a vibrant alternative scene, and a number of seriously hip new indie bands emerge in Bangkok each year. How can one city's music scene be so consistently and annoyingly cool?! The cover art alone on albums by indie labels like Bakery would impress the folks at *Surface* or *Spin* magazines, and the music behind the packaging can be equally cutting-edge. Bands like Modern Dog (pictured here) have become so popular they've almost lost their indie cred. Then again, indie music these days can mean just about anything *not* produced by the two music industry giants – Grammy and RS Promotion.

FAT radio on FM 104.5 is the unofficial home of indie music on the Bangkok airwaves, and insanely popular among high school and college students. Dedicated followers are known as *dek Fat* (kids of Fat), and they'll rarely miss programs like Bedroom Studio, which features debut airings of demo tapes sent in by aspiring college bands.

While Bangkok indie bands have mastered the requisite dumpy appearance and eccentric image, when it comes to lyrics few venture beyond the usual themes of love and longing. One notable exception is a popular indie group conveniently called Rean Cheon Than Poo Mee Chit Sat Tar ('Step Forward Faithful Ones') who cover religious and Buddhist themes like nirvana (the existential state, not the Seattle-based grunge band).

Indie music is part of a larger youth culture scene centered around the many funky shops of Siam Square. Try Underground, a leftist bookshop near the Scala Theater, or the always teeming DoReMe music store and the endless maze of second-hand clothing stalls at Chatuchak market (see "Chatuchak"). It's an interesting juxtaposition: These kids try hard to stand out as 'alternative' but usually come from perfectly good homes, attend university, and don't attribute much meaning to their carefully-faded Che Guevara T-shirts. For all the imagery and the noble search for individuality, true rebelliousness just isn't particularly cool in Thai culture.

The word, we're reminded in so many pop culture essays in the Asia edition of *Time* magazine, is Japanese for 'empty orchestra'. In Bangkok it might as well translate as 'plush, overcrowded room full of over-energetic teens vying for the microphone and howling offensive boy band tunes'. True Bangkok karaoke fiends know how to choose the kind of sappy numbers that would make most normal people physically ill. But the die-hards croon like they mean it, and karaoke in Bangkok is more about the uninhibited social atmosphere than the vomit-inducing music.

Karaoke is particularly popular amongst Bangkok teens on routine mall outings and businessmen looking to wind down after work with whiskey and a girl or three. So widespread is the pastime these days that even some taxis (like that driven by Khun Wichian, pictured here) offer passengers a chance to sing their way to a dreaded dentist appointment.

For Bangkok high school and university students, karaoke is no longer a special event but a quick stop between movies, snacks at the food court and frantic visits to the public toilet. Indeed, the top floor of MBK shopping center (see "MBK") boasts a state-of-the-art karaoke center that includes a whopping seventy-eight private booths with jukeboxes churning out songs at B20 (around 50 cents) a go.

Serious karaoke lounges are typically divided into private 'living rooms' of various sizes, rented by the hour. There's normally a three-hour minimum charge, but it's amazing how time flies when you're belting out heart-on-the-sleeve renditions of 'Careless Whisper' and 'Sleeping Child'. Shoes come off, sofas are leapt upon, and menus strewn around the room offer beer and food and a huge selection of songs in Thai, English and Mandarin. Patrons select tunes via remote control from automated computers that spin DVDs.

Some of Bangkok's more posh establishments offer live karaoke on stage courtesy of an in-house band. Naughty lounges, mainly in upscale massage parlors along Ratchadaphisek Road, include Jacuzzis and attached bedrooms (for those who can't sing but whose talents presumably lie elsewhere). Simpler, street-level karaoke joints, nearly always bathed in garish pink or green fluorescent lights, can be found on nearly any residential side street in Bangkok – usually just a friendly bar where neighbors sing, drink and hang out with the staff.

It is commonly assumed that *kathoey*, or transgenders, are fully accepted in Thai society. It's true to an extent, for they've always played a role in traditional theater and these days often work as actresses, make-up artists and hair stylists. But the road to mainstream acceptance can be bumpier than poorly-crafted silicone implants: Few transsexuals ever land jobs in government, banks, large companies or schools.

One *kathoey* personality who achieved national television fame is Kitmanoch Rojanaasp, known as Khru Lilly ('Teacher Lilly'). A gifted Thai language teacher, she runs a popular tutorial school in Siam Square and hosts a five-minute daily TV program teaching kids Thai grammar in a fun, carefree style.

Another well-known *kathoey* is Nong Toom, who as a male kick-boxer in the 1990s caused a stir by wearing lipstick in the ring and declaring his desire to accumulate enough prize money to fund a sex-change operation. After the surgery she was prohibited from fighting men.

Kathoey from provinces around Thailand flock to Bangkok for jobs that help earn them the $1,200 needed for sex-change surgery. Many are employed as sex workers, while a glamorous few get to star in Bangkok's famous drag shows. A bar on Nana Plaza's second floor is staffed entirely by drop-dead-gorgeous women, all of whom used to be frustrated men. *Kathoey* are so common in Thailand that the Thai Foreign Ministry once considered introducing a new passport format for post-operation transsexuals, bearing two photos: 'before' and 'after'.

In the big city, *kathoey* rely on an extensive sisterhood network with a rich sub-culture. Their slang is documented in The Kathoey Dictionary, and almost every example begins with the exclamation '*tai*' ('die', meaning, "I'm dying, dying!") suggesting the high level of campness required for most situations. Other gems: The English word 'she' is used for the third person, usually in a negative sense, as in "*She phuut arai wa*" ("What the hell did she say?"). 'Mama', a popular instant noodle brand, is a code for pubic hair. Many of these terms have been adopted by trendy young Bangkokians, too.

An important milestone for the Thai tranny community was the 2001 film 'The Iron Ladies'. The box office hit told the true story of a volleyball team comprising *kathoey*, homosexuals and their lesbian coach that managed against all odds to make it to the finals

KHAOSAN ROAD

ถนนข้าวสาร

Since the release a few years ago of a certain Hollywood film featuring a certain Hollywood heartthrob roaming Khaosan Road's busy sidewalks, nearly every media account of Bangkok's backpacker strip has milked this anecdote dry by suggesting that silver-screen exposure "changed the street forever."

In fact Khaosan Road has been undergoing a dramatic transformation since the mid-1990s that has little to do with Leo and far more with the unstoppable forces of market globalization. What started in the early 1980s as a convenient refueling station for cash-strapped ex-hippies is now one of the hippest corners of Bangkok, not just for international travelers but increasingly for Thai students and yuppies as well.

Thai noodle and pancake vendors compete for precious space with gourmet coffee outlets and Western fast food chains; two-dollar-a-night guesthouses are being overtaken by multi-story hotels with gleaming lobbies and rooftop swimming pools; and the experience of queuing for much-anticipated mail at the local *poste restante* is but a distant memory in the wired environment of Kaosan's countless air-conditioned cyber cafés. Some internet shops boast computer keyboards in Korean, Japanese and Hebrew – an internationalization mirrored just outside by swanky food stalls serving up sushi, hummus and falafel. And the street's most recent incarnation as a pedestrian promenade means no more tuk-tuks jamming the road to round up victims for gem shop tours or Patpong go-go bars.

It's easy to knock Khaosan as a cliché of itself or a worn-out backpacker bubble, but we find ourselves coming back fairly often and we're hardly ever disappointed by the buzz. Khaosan, in turn, seems to keep reinventing itself, mostly for the better.

The road remains faithful to a few of its old traditions, however. It is still the street of choice for procuring fake student and journalist IDs, false passports and ESL teaching certificates, braided hair, cheap suits, recreational drugs, and that most dangerous of substances – used books.

If the stench weren't so overwhelming, we'd all move into picturesque teak houses by a *khlong* (canal) first thing tomorrow morning. But it's more than just the foul odor and the troops of mosquitoes: We now know *khlong* water fungi can actually be lethal. In 2003, Thai pop star Apichet Kittikorncharoen, better known as 'Big D2B', managed to drive his car into a *khlong* on his way home from a rehearsal. A passerby jumped into the water and saved Big from instant death but not from the fungus, which caused massive hemorrhaging in the singer's brain. He's been healing slowly but it's unclear whether he'll fully recover from the unfortunate plunge.

Surely it's not *that* dirty? Actually, it is. Bangkok's ten million residents produce 2.5 million cubic meters of wastewater per day, of which just 20% is treated. You'll encounter the rest in your neighborhood *khlong*. While fish and plant life disappeared more than a decade ago, human life still floats around somehow and the city's 100 kilometers of *khlong* remain a popular transport alternative for many traffic-weary Bangkokians. Boat passengers guard themselves against droplets and stench with newspapers, office envelopes and bandanas. When a boat approaches from the opposite direction they'll quickly yank up the plastic side curtain to block the oncoming spray of water. There is no official speed limit along Bangkok's *khlong*, making for some pretty harrowing rides and an exciting 'spray factor'.

Khlong houses are an uneven mishmash of traditional Thai dwellings, modest shacks and bland, modern housing blocks. Most private residences have no fence or other tangible boundary and are instead guarded by vicious-looking dogs. Boats are still popular here, and on many *khlong* even the monks arrive by boat to collect their daily alms (see "Tam Boon"). Other, more earthly *khlong* services include a floating bank ("Sorry Sir, your account has been drowned due to of your overdraft"), floating food stalls and waterborne postmen. Our brave postman-on-a-boat friend, Khun Naruepon, insists the dogs guarding *khlong* houses "are a nightmare". He's been bitten a number of times and is still knocked into the water whenever a dog onslaught becomes particularly fierce. Amazingly, *khlong* canine seem unable (or unwilling) to recall a postman they've seen each and every day for over a year.

69

KHLONG TOEY

คลองเตย

Bangkok's infamous Khlong Toey slum is home to around 100,000 people. It's a dejected place that sits on Port Authority land, which is why most of its inhabitants, who arrived here a few decades ago from Thailand's outer provinces, still cannot own their shacks. Many of their children never went to school because to do so required official documents and a registered house. Meanwhile, their neighborhood has become the capital's chief trading ground for hard drugs, particularly methamphetamines (see "Yaa Baa").

We hung out there for a while, sharing a bench and conversation with a few friendly ladies and their young children while cats and dogs ran circles around us. We chatted about poverty, drug dealers, prostitution and alcohol. They told us how they've grown used to the stench and mosquitoes but not the rats. Life in Bangkok's neglected back yard seems so bleak it's hard to imagine that a place like the Emporium shopping mall (see "Emporium") actually exists. "We are Grade-A slum", offered one of the ladies, alluding to the reputation of *Khlong Toey* (meaning 'Pandanus tree canal') in Thailand. Most people only ever hear of it from media reports of police drug busts, gambling dens and gang fights.

But even *Clongue Teuille*, as we like to call it (sounds like a peaceful Parisian suburb at the end of the metro line, *non*?), has its angels. One of them is Reverend Joe Maier, known as Father Joe, an American who came here in 1971 and was appointed parish priest of this mostly forsaken community. He has since established schools, kindergartens, clinics and a hospice for AIDS patients – with no religious agenda, it should be noted. More than 60,000 kids have been through these schools, paying only B10 (around 25 cents) a day. In the Thai press Maier is known as Father Teresa. Today many other NGOs are active in the neighborhood, funded by donors from around the world. In 2003 *Khlong Toey* community radio started broadcasting from a small wooden house and used local residents as DJs. They are all volunteers, and some show up for a shift with their babies in tow. Listeners don't seem to mind.

KRATING DAENG

กระทิงแดง

Energy drinks are probably not the healthiest things on earth. But if you've ever witnessed your *tuk-tuk* driver nod off to sleep in the middle of a sharp turn into Ploenchit Avenue, you might see a redeeming quality in those punchy little bottles.

Red Bull's official website plugs its controversial syrupy-sweet brew as the drink "for when a long day is over and a long night starts," and "for long, sleep-inducing motorways." No wonder its Thai originator, *Krating Daeng*, is the beverage of choice for so many of Bangkok's groggy-eyed taxi, *motosai* and *tuk-tuk* drivers. Sometimes dubbed 'the poor man's coffee of Asia', *Krating Daeng* (Thai for 'red forest buffalo') originated in Bangkok in the early eighties.

In recent years the beverage shifted up-market to win over yuppies across Asia, from 'E'-popping ravers in Jakarta to workaholic dot-comers in Bangalore. But it has long been available at practically any Bangkok supermarket, convenience store or drink stand, and its real customer base remains the many long-haul truckers and cabbies struggling through twenty-hour shifts.

Nasty rumors have dogged the manufacturer for years: that the stuff is made from bull semen; that it's an ecstasy-type stimulant; that it contains amphetamine. In reality, *Krating Daeng* is a very potent mix of taurin (an amino acid that kick-starts the metabolism), caffeine, sugar and vitamin B. Competing Asian 'health tonics' – Carabao Daeng (launched by popular Thai folk singer Ad Carabao), Lipovitan or M-150 for instance – contain similar mixtures.

Energy drinks constitute a lucrative market in Thailand. Typical battlefields between mega brands are Thai boxing events and rock concerts – industries that are practically funded on the back of energy drink sponsorship.

These strange bottled potions offer a sensation that in some ways reflects Bangkok itself, a wonderful 'high' that comes with a great buzz, only to fade rather quickly, leaving you feeling drained.

LAND OF SMILES

ตนกำเนิดจริง

Welcome to the Land of Smiles! Relax and let the friendly natives pamper you with their unrivaled hospitality, gentle ways, gracious manners and timeless traditions…Take in Bangkok's spectacular monuments, its glistening temples and beautiful handicrafts…See the Rose Garden and the Snake Farm! Cruise the glorious Chao Phraya River and return to a bygone era, an era when Anna Leonowens strutted her stuff along these banks, an era of bullock carts and colorful parasols and endless waterways, an era when every market was a floating market, when every maiden wore silk and orchids and Jim Thompson had not yet disappeared…*Sawatdii*!

Home to a particularly colorful, ornamental culture, Thailand falls victim to a dazzling array of stomach-churning clichés, most aimed at drawing ever more visitors to the kingdom each year. 'Land of Smiles' began as a tourism promotion slogan but has come to symbolize Thailand's marketing of itself in over-romanticized terms. The images probably entice certain kinds of package tourists from Europe but miss an important point: The *real* Bangkok is more intriguing and beautiful at nearly every level than the exoticized City of Angels of tourism brochures.

We've found it's always the uncontrolled, unplanned experiences that make Bangkok – or any place, really – more memorable and better understood. Take a stroll through Chulalongkorn campus and chat with students; hop on a random bus and go wherever it takes you, not knowing where you'll end up or how you'll return; do the same with a longtail boat into Thonburi's network of *khlong*. Walk into that live music café where you see only Thais, and soak up the atmosphere. Spend some quiet time in a small neighborhood Buddhist *wat* (temple), certainly a more personal experience than being herded through the Grand Palace and Temple of the Emerald Buddha. Join a group of elderly *T'ai Chi* exercisers at 6 AM in Lumphini Park. Try strange new kinds of street food instead of just the sumptuous international buffet at the hotel. Rather than buying into 'Amazing Thailand', go out and see amazing Bangkok for what it is – smiles, frowns, humidity and all.

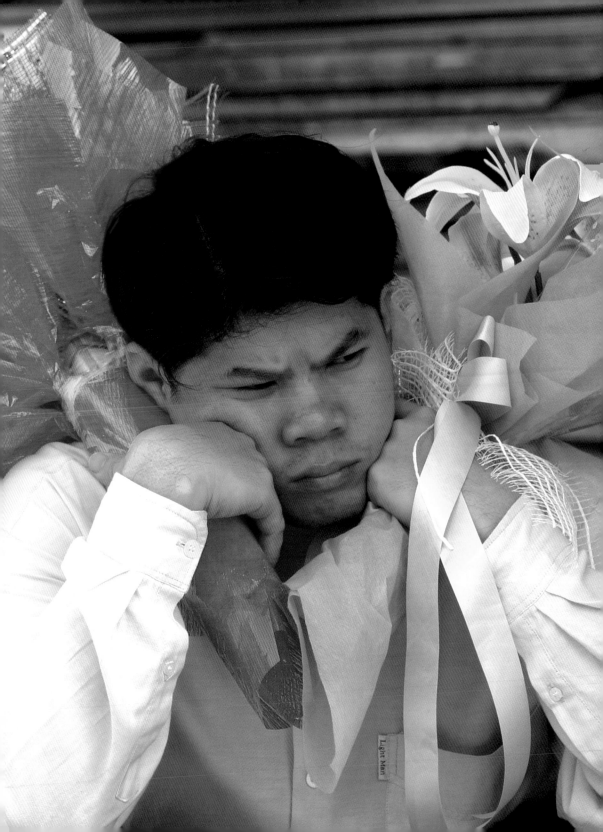

Silence descends on Bangkok. Birds stop flying. *Motosai* drivers cease playing chess with beer bottle caps. Soi dogs do not move (Oops, they never move). It's the crescendo of two weeks of rumors, commotion, hopes and dreams: time for the live TV and radio broadcast of the bi-weekly lottery draw, a Thai national obsession since its inception in 1939.

The lottery (commonly called *Huay*), is held on the 1ˢᵗ and 16ᵗʰ of every month. Over two thirds of the whopping 92 million tickets printed each month are sold in Bangkok.

The draw is held at the Government Lottery Office (GLO) on Ratchadamnern Road, which on the days preceding the big event is teeming with bystanders who queue for discounted last minute tickets. Eleven guests – sometimes beauty queens or other VIPs – pull the lever to reveal the numbered plastic balls, altering the lives of people across the kingdom.

If you miss the live broadcast, find out whether you've snagged the B3 million (about $75,000) grand prize via mobile phone messaging service, the internet or the traditional medium, *Riang Bur* – a leaflet listing the winning numbers – sold by street vendors hours after the draw.

Methods for guessing the magic numbers? Dream interpretation is big and manuals for deciphering dreams are found in virtually any Bangkok bookstore. Some punters resort to supernatural power: Thais usually perceive spirits who live in trees to be 'good spirits', so a rumor that a woman in traditional Thai dress walked into a tree or that a tree yielded something unusual (a fruit shaped like a human head, for instance), means people will gather around that tree, scratch its trunk and supplicate until marks appear that resemble numbers. The ritual is so widespread it has become an idiom – *kood ton mai khor huay* ('scrubbing a tree for lucky numbers'). Variations of this practice include searching for lucky numbers by staring at albino catfish or at the pattern of two-headed gecko.

Monks are popular informants, too. They either speak in cryptic tongues or drop melted candle wax into a bowl of sacred water until it solidifies into subliminal hints. The royal family and other symbols of authority, like mayors, can unknowingly inspire number picks through their birthdays or car license plates, for instance.

Tabloids love reporting on poor folk who win the lottery only to squander their fortune within a short time, a tendency so common it spurred yet another idiom, *Sarm lor took huay* ('Lottery winning *tuk-tuk* driver').

79

LUMPHINI

สวนลุมพินี

If Bangkok sometimes feels like a polluted, claustrophobic prison, Lumphini Park is the fenced outdoor courtyard where each day inmates are alloted precious time to exercise, dance, lift weights, eat, sing, play chess or snooze under a tree.

Suan Lumphini is the city's proverbial 'green lung', a desperately needed oasis in a landscape marked by concrete sky train stations, modern office buildings and fifteen hundred square kilometers of half-finished urban sprawl. If the Chao Phraya River is Bangkok's unlikely waterfront, Lumphini is its makeshift forest and wannabe lake.

Few places we've seen around the world are as genuinely public as this. People of all ages and backgrounds come here to Rollerblade, enjoy a family picnic, paddle a boat, aerobicize or just contemplate nature for a while. And Bangkokians harbor a true sense of ownership over Lumphini. Local government once tried to close the park to the public so that visiting Australian PM John Howard could jog there, but protests by outraged residents forced authorities to nix the plan.

The park is particularly refreshing because while the city's shopping malls are dominated by bleeping, vibrating, consumption-driven teens, Lumphini is largely the domain of an older, more introspective generation. Many of the early morning *T'ai Chi* exercise groups, comprising mostly elderly Chinese-Thais, have been performing the same graceful motions together each and every dawn for decades. Some practice tango dancing at the park's senior citizen community center. Others wile away the afternoon huddled around chess tables, outwitting each other at a snail's pace under the shade of tamarind trees. Those with a bit more energy pump iron at the open-air gyms.

Lumphini is also a favorite pre-office breakfast stop for workers heading to the nearby Silom business district. Stalls selling delicious porridge, *khao tom* (boiled rice), fruit drinks, coconut pudding, *dim sum* and other snacks line the park's main entrances and open-air food court. In the cool season, Lumphini hosts a series of delightful outdoor classical music concerts. Less forgiving on the ears are the many karaoke stalls playing Chinese oldies. The singing is spine-chillingly bad and the amplifiers far too powerful for public well-being.

Lumphini's daytime activity ends each evening when park-goers stand at attention for the Thai national anthem. After hours, the action moves outside the park fence, where prostitutes of all persuasions solicit prospective clients.

In Thailand's volatile economy, the safest kind of pension plan works like this: If you are Caucasian, marry a Thai and have some kids; if you are Thai, procreate with a Caucasian. The result will be much-desired *Luuk Kreung*, or mixed-race children. In modern Thailand such offspring are regarded as the best invention since *yam plaa duuk fuu* crispy catfish salad. Through advertising jobs, talk show hosting gigs, constant attention in the gossip tabloids and mostly mediocre singing careers, *Luuk Kreung* kids are virtually guaranteed to serve as family cash cows for years to come.

Willy McIntosh (pictured here) is of Thai-British lineage and among the earliest *Luuk Kreung* stars to make it big as a Bangkok celebrity. This actor, TV presenter and businessman is a household name in Thailand. Miraculously, Willy's sister, Kathaleeya McIntosh, is *also* a successful actress and TV presenter, and the siblings were chosen as Thailand's sexiest people in a Durex global sex survey.

The popular obsession with *Luuk Kreung* (literally 'half child') exemplifies the seemingly paradoxical identity of many young Thais in this modern age. They dream globally, pepper their speech with trendy English-language phrases, worship foreign pop icons and consumer brands and crave a lighter skin tone. Yet they wish to remain true to their roots and home. In a recent survey Thai teens were asked to name the world's best place to live and overwhelmingly chose Thailand. In *Luuk Kreung* kids, Thais find an exotic and sometimes enviable degree of foreignness, but also a recognizable part of themselves.

Luuk Kreung are a wide-ranging phenomenon. Some grew up overseas and hardly speak a word of Thai, while others are Thai-born and bred, went to local schools and have little to do with the outside world aside from genealogy.

Luuk Kreung stars must tread carefully and refrain from 'un-Thai' behavior, or risk falling quickly out of public favor. Even the wildly popular Thai-American teen idol Tata Young proved vulnerable. Her hit song, 'Sexy, Naughty, Bitchy' raised eyebrows at Thailand's Ministry of Culture. When the pop singer recorded with American producers and was seen as becoming 'too confident' in her ways (a big Thai cultural no-no), she took a beating from the press and fans alike.

85

MASSAGE

นวด

The seedy Bangkok massage parlor stereotype is even older than that clichéd song from 'Chess', but the city today boasts such a wild variety of massage styles that trying to pigeonhole the term is pointless.

The two classic, world-renowned and time-honored methods are of course Traditional Thai Massage (*nuad paen boran*) and the kind variously known as 'Full Body Massage', 'Soapy Tit Massage' or 'Happy Ending'. We'll resist expanding on either genre because every other book on Bangkok already does. But it's the smorgasbord of methods in between these two that never fails to impress.

Popular massage indulgences offered in Bangkok include Japanese Shiatsu, Chinese Acupuncture, Swedish Aromatherapy, Balinese Oil Rub, Foot Reflexology, Herbal Wrap, Body Scrub and, our most recent favorite, Doggie Style (not what you think, but rather what you see in this photo).

This latest massage service, introduced by veteran Bangkok dog breeder Anupun Boonchoen, aims to relieve your debilitated pooch from tension associated with his or her fast-paced urban existence. Khun Anupun's masseurs and masseuses were trained in traditional Thai massage and spent over a thousand hours treating humans before undergoing a special dog massage course. But Anupun has found that dogs with anxiety issues generally had problematic owners, so a one-hour deep kneading session with aromatic oil rubbed around the ears won't necessarily remedy the situation for some unfortunate mutts.

The city's elaborate massage possibilities extend to the choice of venues, too. Unlike primitive, less indulgent Western societies, Bangkok massage spots run the socio-economic gamut. Get a good traditional pummeling anywhere from simple neighborhood salons and shopping centers to airport lounges, budget backpacker haunts, executive night clubs or world class luxury spas. A while back, one of the city's leading petrol station chains offered quick-relax massage treatments to its drive-thru customers.

86

In Bangkok, it is fair to say, the medium is the massage.

In a city that resembles a real-life Shopping Channel, Mahboonkrong Center, known as MBK, represents the quintessential Bangkok shopping experience. With seven cacophonous floors of consumer frenzy, over 1,000 shops and some 100,000 eager visitors per day, MBK is where the Thai street bazaar meets the trendy mega-mall.

MBK's strength is value for money and the availability of simply everything. Great deals can be had on punk boots and mobile phone accessories, pirated DVDs and three-hour facial treatments, custom-made stickers and vintage cameras, retro clothing, camping gear and, literally, kitchen sinks. And its proximity to Chulalongkorn University means the shops stay keenly abreast of the very latest fashion and gadget trends. It also merits distinction as the city's most chaotic space that is fully air-conditioned.

MBK's biggest pitfall is that Sunday afternoons are so overcrowded that an obvious Next Big Thing for some budding Thai entrepreneur would be to introduce oxygen bars on each floor. Many venues already provide temporary respite from the madness, offering soothing foot massages, private karaoke booths or conveyor-belt feasts of sushi and green tea. MBK isn't for all tastes. Rich kids (see "Hi-So/Lo-So") and Bangkok society ladies tend to look down on it as an unseemly place – a low-end human zoo far too chaotic for comfort.

Mahboonkrong first opened its doors in 1984, the name a hybrid honoring the developer's parents, Ma Bulkul and Boonkrong. The endearing thing about MBK is how true it remains to its original character despite many shifting trends, a dramatic 1996 fire and rather frequent renovations. For all the high-tech bleeps emerging from the 4th-floor gadget section, artisans on the ground floor still painstakingly labor away at custom-ordered oil portraits; a stall selling 1930s classical Thai music remains popular as ever; and the Slush Puppy drink machine behind the main entrance escalator hasn't moved an inch since we first came here in 1991.

89

Thailand's historical knack for embracing foreign influences while safeguarding a strong, homegrown identity was a key to avoiding colonization when its neighbors were being overrun by foreign powers. Bangkok has never been afraid of hosting a colorful assortment of ethnic groups, and is growing more heterogeneous by the year.

So cosmopolitan is the city these days that for all the foreign faces and accents, Central Bangkok sometimes feels more like London or New York than a Thai city. And like in so many other global hubs, different ethnic groups park themselves comfortably in certain parts of town. When we crave hummus at 2 AM, it's nice to have the Middle Eastern enclave of Soi Nana (see "Nana"). When it's a cup of *chai* or Bollywood DVDs we seek, our helicopter pilot knows the quickest route to Pahurat, Bangkok's charming little piece of India. *Kimchi* cravings can be addressed near Sukhumvit Soi 8, where a shopping complex caters to the city's 18,000-strong Korean community and boasts a Korean church, Korean comic shops and Korean supermarkets. *Borscht* aficionados, however, must head down the coast to Pattaya, apparently the Russian hangout of choice.

The Chinese are the city's biggest and oldest minority, and its most integrated, too. While the Yaowarat district (see "Chinatown") is the city's Chinese cultural hub, Chinese influence has profoundly shaped Bangkok as a whole and can be felt absolutely everywhere.

Around 50,000 Japanese live in Bangkok and their Little Tokyo is centered around Sukhumvit Soi 33/1, an alley lined with Japanese executive clubs, hair salons, travel agencies, bookshops, restaurants and even flower arrangement schools. Nightclubs along Soi Thaniya in Patpong cater exclusively to Japanese *salarimen*, and the glamorous hostesses out front (all of whom speak basic Japanese and bow like undernourished geishas) focus so exclusively on their niche that they won't even glance at a non-Japanese passerby.

Not all ethnic groups enjoy such glamour. Indians and Pakistanis, known locally as *kaek*, encounter informal discrimination within Bangkok society. The city is also an adopted home for workers from neighboring countries like Burma, Cambodia and Laos. Some are officially employed, usually as housekeepers, factory workers and manual laborers, but the majority work illegally. Many are essentially bonded laborers in the sex industry or the manufacturing sector, living in terrible conditions and without access to basic health services.

MOBILE PHONES

ब द्य बेग्ड

If you've wondered what cellular techies have been slaving away for in R&D labs all these years, witness how their technology is applied each and every day in Bangkok:

Jom: "Hello, Kwan!"

Kwan: "Watdii kha, Jom. How are things?"

Jom: "Alright, I'm with Ton, Ae and Je in MBK. Where are you?"

Kwan: "In Siam Discovery, with Oy, Aew and Ai, bored to death. We're so hungry! Ai wants pizza, Aew wants noodles and I want sushi, and Oy has tummy ache and doesn't want to eat. Dunno what to do."

Jom: "OK, I'll call or text you again soon to see what's new."

Yes, Bangkok *meu teu* (mobile phone) communication typically consists of food and bowel movement updates for a globalized era, a plethora of monosyllabic, tonal nicknames, and no point whatsoever.

Around half the city's residents own a *meu teu* and the figure increases each day. So eager are mobile phone providers to nab new subscribers that one provider recently offered a special SMS package for the deaf, who until then had somehow evaded the cellular phone industry's aggressive marketing arm. Favorite customers are undoubtedly the bookies at Thai kickboxing stadiums. They wrap themselves in belts that hold up to a hundred phones, barking the odds to multiple clients in faraway villages.

Bangkok's *meu teu* Mecca is MBK shopping center's fourth floor – a dizzying cacophony of loud bleeps and frantic lights where people buy and sell handsets, acquire spare parts or perform 'facelifts' on existing models in an effort to keep up with trends. Bangkok ringtones are loud, obnoxious and mercilessly long. Often it's a tinny, polyphonic rendition of the latest Thai teen pop hit. Spend an hour at MBK's *meu teu* section on a Sunday and you'll require long-term counseling.

Bangkok gals are notorious for their mobile phone interrogation technique. They call their men and ask: "Where are you? What are you doing? Who are you with? Why? When are you coming home?" We propose coding these questions as 1, 2, 3, 4 and 5, respectively, in an effort to save everyone lots of time.

Meu-teu once played a more profound role in Bangkok, during 1992 protests aimed at ousting then-Prime Minister Gen. Suchinda Kraprayoon. For the very first time, most demonstrators were from the yuppie middle class. They arrived in their cars and used mobile phones to recruit supporters, thus the term '*mob meu teu*' ('mobile phone demonstration') was born.

MONARCHY

ราชาธิปไตย

On a nighttime stroll along Bangkok's Champs Elysées, Ratchadamnern Avenue, one cannot help but notice the huge, brightly lit portraits of royal family members. This is when Bangkok truly feels like the capital city of a kingdom.

Bangkokians, like all Thais, hold HM King Bhumibol Adulyadej in great esteem and regard him as a protective father figure and unifying force that transends day-to-day politics. There is hardly a shop in Bangkok that does not display a framed picture of His Majesty – portrayed with his family, toting his Canon camera on a visit to a remote village, or as a young boy. And Thais still maintain a special place in their hearts for the legendary King Chulalongkorn, or Rama V (depicted on this talisman). Indeed, the monarchy's adoring subjects surround themselves so completely with royal imagery that shops selling portraits of Thai monarchs are found in nearly every neighborhood. Even mobile food carts are often smothered in stickers portraying royal figures, and just outside town, the country's biggest amusement park doesn't use imaginary characters as mascots; instead, images of the country's beloved King and Queen loom large over the entrance gate.

King Bhumibol, born in 1927, is the ninth monarch of the 223-year-old Chakri dynasty, and ascended the throne in 1946. He is married to Queen Sirikit and they have three daughters and one son. The royal family is constantly engaged in social welfare initiatives, mainly in rural Thailand. These range from imparting vocational skills to impoverished villagers or introducing new crops and irrigation systems, to preserving Thai arts and music. Each evening, TV stations broadcast summaries of royal family activities that day, whether it was the inauguration of a new development project or attendance at an important Buddhist ceremony. This is an opportunity to hear 'Royal Thai': verbs and formulae used only in a royal context, and flawless diction that includes a distinction between the 'r' and 'l' sounds rarely practiced in Thai these days.

Thais also demonstrate reverence to their monarch through the royal anthem (distinct from the national anthem) played to a standing audience before any movie screening. Different cinema chains in Bangkok use different video clips and musical arrangements for the anthem. This is why our friend Pen will watch films strictly at the Major Cineplex chain, which boasts the most moving royal anthem presentation. When we dare to catch a film at a different cinema, we need to keep it a secret from her.

94

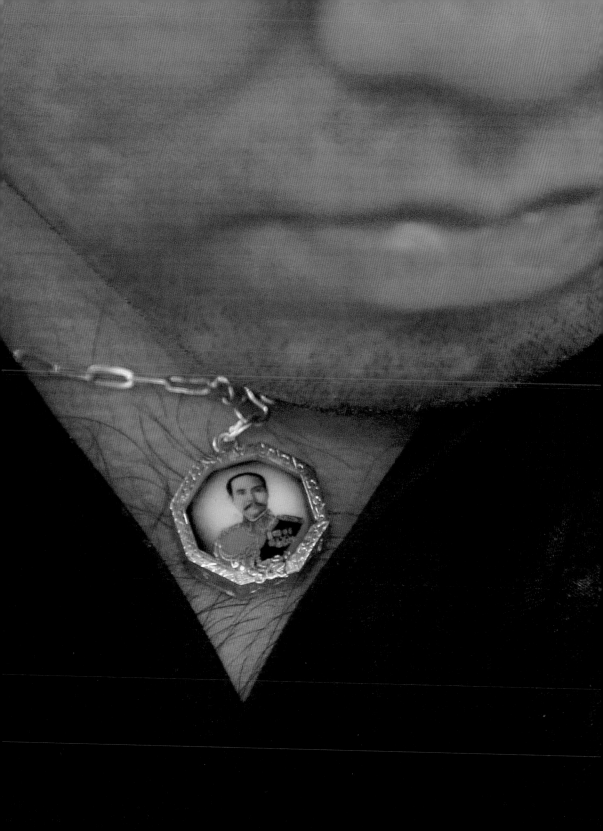

The quickest and arguably most dangerous way to move around Bangkok during rush hour is to hop on a motorcycle taxi. An estimated 200,000 *motosai* drivers ply the roads of Bangkok, organized through 4,500 neighborhood stalls where they can be found busily playing chess, reading tabloids, gossiping and sleeping. Nobody knows quite how, but from a state of total slumber they can be ready in seconds to whisk you to your destination, squeezing their vehicle through rows of cars, *tuk-tuk* and fume-emitting buses. It usually costs less than a taxi and true Bangkokians will know precisely how much to pay their *motosai* guy on a given route. Some passengers even have a regular driver report to their their home at exactly the same hour each morning.

Motosai drivers march to their own beat. They'll stop abruptly in the middle of the road to take a mobile phone call from their girlfriend who's demanding to know what they're doing ("Driving a passenger!"). They'll hit 100km/h and burst out laughing when you plead with them to slow down, and they'll ask your opinion of Thai women before demanding to hear all about your sex life. About 3% of *motosai* drivers, incidentally, are female.

Drivers zip around town in bright orange vests that bear their stall name and registration number. Most are migrants from Isaan (see *"Chao Isaan"*) and earn about B300-600 (around $8-15) a day, of which they must pay a daily fee of B70-100 to the stall boss. They also pay a hefty 'vest fee' of B4,000-20,000 (around $100-500) to join a stall in the first place. If you thought Thais were always a peaceful bunch, witness a foolhardy attempt by a *motosai* driver to steal a passenger from another stall's turf. It's a *faux pas* that carries potentially lethal consequences.

All told, it's a lucrative industry. Annual revenues are estimated at $480 million, of which a quarter is extortion money extracted by police and local politicians from *motosai* ringleaders.

MUAY THAI

มวยไทย

The brash, outrageously colored boxing shorts that hang from souvenir stalls around the city hint at the roaring atmosphere of a *Muay Thai* (Thai kickboxing) match. A live *Muay Thai* bout is a true assault on the senses – certainly more so than the go-go stunts performed at any Patpong bar.

While the *Muay Thai* fight itself can be utterly captivating, the real magic is in the energy that charges through the arena the moment things start to heat up. A tense duel combined with frantic betting in the stands, scantily clad models hoisting placards that announce each round and wailing notes of a Thai *phii chawa* (oboe) that seem to mirror the fighters' nervous prance all combine for a pretty cool way to kill a few Bangkok hours.

Muay Thai is a highly ritualized affair. Trainers bless their fighters before a match begins and contestants wear a Buddha image on their armband for divine protection. Upon entering the ring, boxers bow in the direction of their birthplace and perform the *Wai Khru* ('teacher salute') – a dance tribute to trainers, parents and ancestors.

When the bell sounds, fighters abandon cultural niceties and proceed to pummel the crap out of each other with their knees, elbows, fists and legs. Other than the groin, no target is out of bounds. Fiery matches result in plenty of blood (mind your clothes if you're sitting ringside) and the occasional ring death. Still, *Muay Thai* is the world's fastest-growing contact sport.

The *Muay Thai* of major arenas – like Bangkok's Lumphini and Ratchadamnern stadiums – is a glamorous event followed live on national TV by millions of devoted fans. But the grassroots *Muay Thai* of neighborhood gyms has migrant, working-class, roots and an equally dedicated following. Aspiring kick boxers live and train in local gyms and submit to a rigorous regime of fitness and discipline. Only a lucky, talented few ever get to bask in the Lumphini spotlight.

For a gruesome, no-holds-barred view of the action, splurge on ringside seats at either of the big stadiums. The frenetic gambling action amongst spectators and bookies is best viewed from the cheap seats at the back. The strange men draped in large holsters and a web of wires have the fashion sense of Gaza Strip suicide bombers but are in fact just friendly bookies. They each operate as many as 100 mobile phones simultaneously, providing live, blow-by-blow odds to clients around the country.

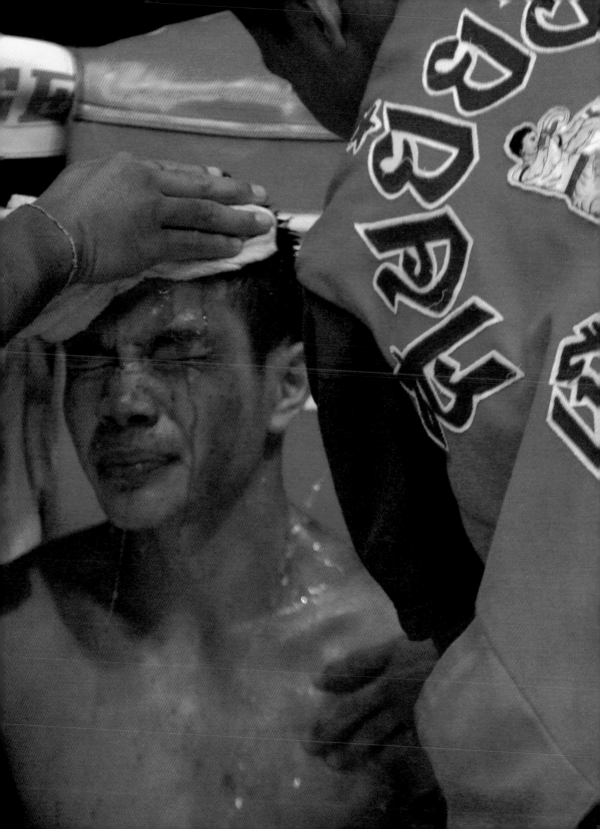

The cluster of alleyways around Sukhumvit Soi 3, or Soi Nana, is an exceptionally vibrant, colorful place for two reasons. It's where Africa meets Arabia (see "My Grace Hotel Weekend") and it's where a whole lot of foreign men meet a whole lot of bar girls. Since the two worlds aren't necessarily connected, Nana is a chaotic scene indeed. After a few hours spent wandering these bustling back alleys, most people need to head straight home for a good rest.

The city's substantial Arab and African populations converge here, and Nana's shops cater almost exclusively to the tastes of merchants from Cameroon and Nigeria, Kuwait, Bahrain and Qatar. Outdoor bars provide cold beer, live Al-Jazeera broadcasts and entrancing Congolese music; streetside *shawarma* vendors carve succulent lamb into *pita* bread at B50 (around $1.25) a pop; overseas phone offices advertise cut-rate prices on calls to Senegal, Sudan and Saudi Arabia; restaurant patrons take long drags from *shisha* pipes after enjoying a meal of *tabouleh* salad and fried pigeon; and hole-in-the-wall travel agents hawk discounted tickets with Ethiopian Airlines, Egypt Air and Emirates, while changing money on the side. The Middle Eastern food here is easily the best in the city, and if you ever want to meet people from twenty different countries in just under an hour, this little enclave is Bangkok's very own outdoor United Nations.

Right across Sukhumvit Road and a few hours after dark, another scene unfolds. Nana Entertainment Plaza's three raucous floors of go-go bars and neon glare keep the mostly Western male clientele amused and intoxicated until the wee hours (or until whatever hour the government's ever-evolving Social Order Policy allows on a given month). Right outside the Plaza is a signature late-night Bangkok brew of love hotels, ladyboys, liquor stores, pharmacies, hookers, taxi stands, fast food joints and body massage parlors, guaranteeing that obese, sweaty, drunken white men need not waddle more than a block or two to satisfy every carnal desire. If you've come to Southeast Asia hoping to witness a truly exotic culture, look no further.

It's with great hesitation that we include Patpong in here, because this so-called red light district is hardly the 'Must See' attraction of guidebook hype, and is in any case covered ad nauseam in nearly every piece of literature on the city.

We won't waste your time discussing its fascinating history, intriguing social undercurrents or the sad stories of the women who work here. Enough writers have conducted comprehensive 'research' on the place and produced an 'interesting' body of work on the topic (our favorite is the timeless classic, *Hello My Big Big Honey*).

Bottom line: Patpong is today one of Bangkok's least exciting nightspots. Perhaps the only amusing thing left to do here is observe tour buses of fat retired European women descend on the street with mischievous, giddy expressions that suggest they think they are about to see or do something very, very naughty. Granted, old Helga might get to glimpse a firm titty or two, or witness that unspeakable trick with the ping pong ball ("Look Bertha, she's doing it! *Ach du lieber Gott*! Tee hee hee!") but that's pretty much what Patpong has become: a broken record and tired tourist attraction about as hip and exciting as London's Madame Tussauds wax museum on a Wednesday afternoon.

Ironically, Patpong is a pretty good place to take the whole family shopping – as long as you don't mind exposing your nine-year-old daughter to sidewalk signs that scream *Pussy Show!* ("It's like a circus with cats, dear, but it's closed today.") Stalls selling handicrafts, fake brand name goods, DVDs and children's toys far outnumber the girlie bars and Turkish Saunas. There's some great street food to be had in the vicinity and even a McDonald's at each end of the strip.

An innocent ten-minute stroll through Bangkok's streets sometimes ends up feeling like a three-hour walk through a large furnace room. Breathing grows difficult, traffic fumes find a new home on your face, and those salty beads of sweat fogging your eyes begin to really sting. You could seek refuge in a branch of Bangkok's favorite air-con convenience chain (See "7-Eleven"), but in the unlikely event that there isn't one just around the corner, try Bangkok's idea of a cold shower-on-the-run, the *pha yen*.

Like the less-is-more Buddhist philosophy, *pha yen* is a simple thing that can – for a few moments at least – alter your existential state. *Pha yen* – meaning 'cold cloth' – come wrapped in a tight plastic pouch and look like something between a *Wet One*™ and those cold freshen-up towels served on airplanes. They're available at virtually any streetside mom-and-pop store in the city, and kept in the coldest corner of the chrome-and-glass fridge so that the towel is still icy enough to shock one's nervous system upon first contact with the flesh.

The easiest way to break open the plastic wrapping is with a resolute, almost violent clap of the hands. This produces a loud bang that is particularly popular with Bangkok teenagers huddled around tables at family restaurants (see "DIY Dining"). Work the face quickly, though, as *pha yen* are effective for about 26 seconds before evolving from a crisp icicle state to a soggy rag resembling the 32-degree temperature outside.

There are two main types of *pha yen* – expensive and cheap. Pricier ones are made of high-quality cloth, dosed in imported eau-de-toilette and wrapped in beautifully designed aluminum foil packaging. They cost B10-20 (around 25-50 cents) depending on point of sale. The cheaper variety is manufactured at small factories in and around Bangkok, and fetches between B2-5 per piece.

Important Tip: Be sure to pronounce the *pha* with an aspirated 'p' or you'll be asking for a 'cold auntie', interpretations of which could lead to any number of surprising situations in a city like Bangkok.

109

PHARMACIES

ร้านขายยา

Bangkok pharmacies are more than just a place people go for medication. First, they're found on just about any city street corner, outnumbered perhaps only by 7-Elevens, ATMs and fresh jackfruit stalls. Second, many are open 24 hours and stock not just pharmaceuticals but cold drinks and snacks as well. Third, they are substance Disneylands where one can score just about any upper, downer or sedative on the market with no medical prescription whatsoever.

All of this explains why Bangkok pharmacies have practically become hangout venues in their own right – places folks might pop into for a few minutes on the way to a nightclub or the kickboxing stadium, just to snoop around and see what's new on the market. So lax are regulations on prescription drugs here that many foreign visitors to the Thai capital treat local drug outlets as pharmaceutical candy stores.

We spoke to a number of pharmacists in central Bangkok who offered no apologies for the easy availability of their goods, explaining that demand is high and enforcement very weak. Prozac remains a perennial *farang* favorite; B2,400 (about $60) gets you a month's worth of the trendy anti-depressant, but a *fluoxetine* generic version costs just a quarter of that price. Xanax, the popular anti-anxiety sedative, rings in at just B550 (about $14) for 100 capsules in its generic *alprazolam* form.

And considering Bangkok's legendary nightlife, it's not surprising that Viagra is up there on the pharmaceutical bestseller list (original, a somewhat stiff $10 per tablet; generic, a more flaccid $4). "About 80% of Viagra buyers are Japanese," one pharmacist on Silom Road volunteered with a smile and a wink, "I don't know why. Almost always Japanese." Flavored condoms (strawberry sells best) and KY jelly are checkout counter favorites at late-night pharmacies in the city's entertainment districts.

PHRA ATHIT

ถนนพระอาทิตย์

Phra Athit Road along the Chao Phraya River in Bunglamphu is a unique slice of Bangkok that's evolved from Old Town to Indie Central in a few short years. The transition built upon the street's distinctive character rather than displacing it, so Phra Athit today is a delightful stretch of modish bars, pubs, bakeries, bookshops and boutiques, and arguably the city's friendliest nightspot. It's a colorful place, too, thanks to some charming guesthouses (spillovers from nearby Khaosan Road), traditional Chinese noodle shops and majestically restored mansions, like the high-ceilinged Baan Phra Athit, part of which has been converted into a fashionable café.

Equally colorful is the cast of human characters, representing a broad cross-section of Bangkok society. Phra Athit is where the old noodle vendor meets the documentary filmmaker, the office worker encounters the aerobics fanatic, and the intrepid backpacker comes face-to-face with the Thammasat sociology student. Visual artists, multi-media installation buffs, fringe theater actors and fine arts professors with their students all loiter around Phra Athit's bohemian hangouts and dream of Paris-based projects, preferably funded by the EU. Nearby, and hardly by coincidence, lie two of the country's top academic institutions, Thammasat and Silpakorn universities. The former is a breeding ground for future lawyers and politicians, while the latter churns out artists, some of whom end up opening pubs and bars along Phra Athit Road....

The street's cafés, bars and pubs – all traditional shophouses prior to mid-1990s gentrification – are always welcoming and cozy, and some regularly host photography and art exhibitions. Student pubs are low-key affairs that open at night, great for succulent Thai bar snacks and first-rate live folk guitar music (if you're into mellow Thai love songs that make you cry). Groups of university students, sometimes still in uniform, drink cheap whiskey and mixers (see "Whiskey, Coke & Ice") while singing and swaying to the music.

Phra Sumen Fort, built on the old city's outer wall during the reign of King Rama I, stands at the eastern end of the street. The adjacent park, on the river's edge, hosts morning and evening aerobics sessions that draw hundreds of enthusiastic participants. A twilight stroll around here can cleanse the soul. Watching the boats, ferries and barges move along the murky river, we sometimes forget we're in chaotic Bangkok.

Upon hopping into a Bangkok taxi we can always tell whether the driver has just begun his shift or is about to doze off at the wheel. If his *phuangmalai* – the flower garland hung from the rear view mirror – is fresh and fragrant, it means the shift has just started. If it is wilted, the driver is likely drained as well.

Thais buy *phuangmalai* for their cars to protect them against road accidents. According to Buddhist belief, people are protected at home by the good spirit of the house (*jao thii*). Outside they are more vulnerable and so require protection. The sacred flower garlands represent an offering to the good, protective spirits. Such insurance, in the form of a basic streetside *phuangmalai*, usually costs B20 (about 50 cents).

Phuangmalai are commonly prepared by threading white Mali blossoms or Arabic Jasmine on a cord to create a necklace-like garland with two strands of flowers connected by a cotton or banana leaf string. It takes an experienced florist about thirteen minutes to create a fifteen-centimeter garland.

Bangkok is one of the only places in Thailand where flower garlands are sold at traffic intersections, usually by children from nearby slums who thread them at home before plying them on the street. They normally earn B300-500 (about $8-12) per day. During the 2003 APEC summit in Bangkok, the government deemed *phuangmalai* sellers unsightly and banned them from major intersections. Residents were also asked not to place flower garlands on the brand new elephant statues erected around town for the high-profile event.

Phuangmalai are also sold at markets, outside temples and at flower shops. For customers seeking something fancier than the basic garland, the sky is the limit. Folks blessing a new house, new car or new budget airline will arrange for monks to officiate at a ceremony laden with grand, intricately designed flower garlands.

When darkness falls, a single neon bulb beckons drivers to stop and buy garlands at roadside stalls. On rainy nights when hardly anyone ventures out, it's particularly sad to see our *phuangmalai* lady, dispirited and bored, trying desperately to sell her remaining flowers. The pink neon light glows in anguish. The last garlands whisper "Take me…take me…" until a car pulls up – usually a taxi – and its driver secures a pair of garlands for the road. Only then can Ms. Phuangmalai head home for a good night's sleep.

POLLUTION

มลภาวะ

A breath of fresh air for B20? Our weekly special: three particles of oxygen for B3 a piece? Or maybe our unique 'Air du Jour', which today happens to be 'Luzern Express', monsieur? We'll take them all, merci.

Bangkok air quality isn't as bad as it used to be, but the familiar *kwan dam* ('black smoke') we know and love is still firmly in place. A 2002 study estimated that 900,000 Bangkokians suffered from respiratory diseases that year, and that 700 others actually died from bad air.

Committees on air quality come and go, but it's an uphill battle. Bangkokians love to drive, and each year a greater number of new vehicles join the streets, ensuring that a few extra people die from the lethal fumes. As always, those who suffer most from the main pollutant, 'airborne particulate matter', are the poor as they are typically the ones working outdoors.

Things have improved significantly over the last decade, though. In 1996 Thailand switched to unleaded gasoline and at the city's airport, for instance, visibility increased from about 5km in 1996 to 9km by 2000. But the sky train system created another problem – fumes get trapped under the stations. When waiting for a bus under a skytrain station we always face the same dilemma: Shall we remain in place, helplessly inhaling the thick grey fumes, or hop on a *motosai* and risk our lives in a different way? We usually end up choosing a *motosai* ride because we are men and dig the powerful rush that comes with zipping through a busy Bangkok street on the back of a shiny motorbike.

But think of all that we gain from air pollution. Thanks to the haze, the twilight hours can be incredibly eerie and colorful, perfect for pink-hued tourist snapshots of the Chao Phraya River. Turning on the air conditioning when you get home becomes nothing short of orgasmic, and traveling overseas usually means some pretty funky, hallucinatory fits due to all the extra oxygen that suddenly infiltrates the lungs.

If you haven't yet noticed, Bangkokians are masters of euphemism. Ask a local about the air in Bangkok and they'll answer: "It's too hot, I can't stand it." *Hot*, you see, *hot*.

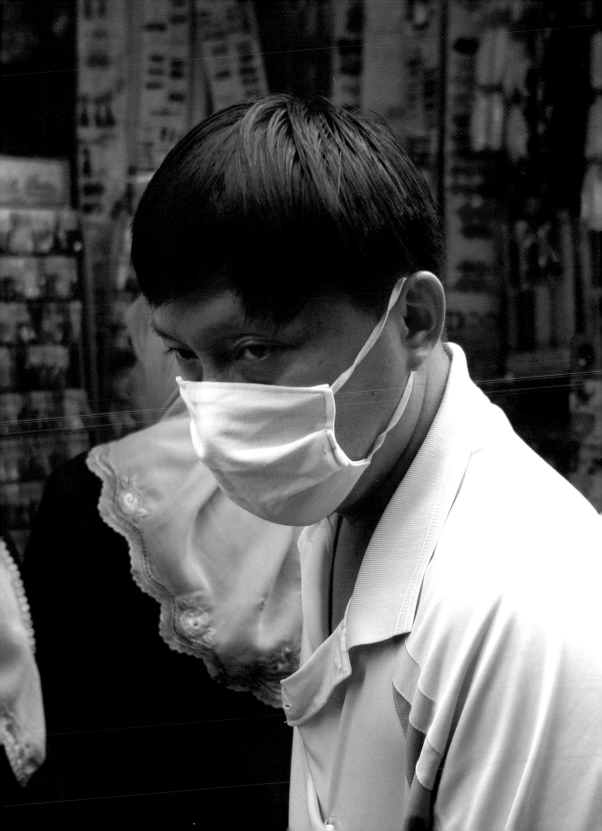

In the concrete jungle that is modern Bangkok, one of our favorite oases is the Raja Hotel on Sukhumvit Soi 4. The hotel lobby is straight out of the 1950s, with old rotary phones, white stone floors, black leather art deco sofas and a doorman so old he might as well be part of the vintage furnishings. A sign at the entrance lists Bangkok destinations served by the hotel's limousine, including the Soviet Embassy and the offices of Air Ceylon and Pan American. Gone are the days when we'd meet Sergei here: He'd sit at the back of the lobby and chain-smoke Gauloises, hold up an issue of *Pravda* and wait for our bi-weekly microfilm, which was hidden, of course, inside an Isaan sausage.

When we contacted the Raja's owner, he was wholly unimpressed with our admiration for his vintage hotel. "It's an old hotel, it's no good", he muttered impatiently before hanging up on us. Unsurprisingly, the Raja is pretty empty these days, but not so the neighboring Atlanta, Miami and Honey hotels in the same neighborhood, which are livelier affairs and offer comparable doses of nostalgia (and some kitsch thrown in for good measure). Chinatown, with its mock-colonial mansions, funky old shophouses and wonderful storefront signs, is also prime hunting ground for retro-spotters.

Sadly, most of Bangkok's majestic old cinema buildings offer little these days besides soft porn, dilapidated lobbies and awful sound systems. Only a few have undergone proper restoration. Bangkok conventional wisdom dictates that "old equals bad" and "new equals good", which is why heritage buildings keep getting torn down for yet more flyovers, apartment buildings or fitness clubs. Only Rattanakosin Island – Bangkok's 'inner city' and historical heart – is strictly off-limit to developers.

While Bangkok retro appreciation is clearly on the upswing, vintage artifacts still attract mainly foreign buyers. A number of dealers at Section 1 in Chatuchak Market sell Thai movie posters from the 1960s, original covers of *Le Petit Journal* from the early 1900s, old photos and postcards of Siam, vintage cameras and radio receivers.

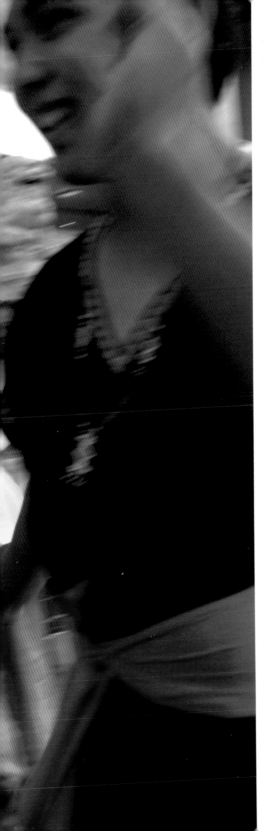

The Thai term *sanuk*, which is sometimes translated as 'fun', is in fact much more nuanced than that. A Bangkokian woman once asked us whether the funeral we just returned from was *sanuk*. It's really about doing things together and about eating, you see. So we answered, "yes."

More conventional *sanuk* activities in Bangkok include wandering aimlessly for hours around Siam Square, watching a film (during the boring parts you chat loudly with friends on your mobile phone), drinking with close mates, slurping noodles at 3 AM on the way home from a huge dinner and sending cute text messages to giggly friends.

Activities conducted alone are by definition not *sanuk* (mind you, the particular activity you're thinking of right now usually *feels* quite *sanuk*). This is why things can potentially get awkward for a *farang* hanging out with a group of Thai friends. Breaking away from the clan after a few hours of window shopping at the mall and mumbling "I think I need some quality time by myself right now" contradicts the essence of *sanuk*-ness. It's an individualist approach alien to the collectivist Thai culture, and doesn't go over too well. This also explains why Thais find room on their calendars to celebrate the Thai New Year, Christian New Year and Chinese New Year, all of which are situations with exceptional *sanuk* potential.

Things you do every day are definitely not *sanuk*. Ditto for visiting places with disappointing shopping and food scenes, like Eastern Europe. Above all, *sanuk* is something that massages the collective senses and leaves everyone with a nice, light, smiley feeling. This is why heavy things, like Wim Wender films, can never be *sanuk*. Legally Blonde, or anything starring Jim Carrey, are.

"*Sanuk mai*" ("Was it *sanuk*?") is one of the most frequently asked questions at any given moment in Bangkok, and answering "*Mai sanuk*" ("No, it wasn't") will usually mean an immediate noodle or drinking session with friends – phase one of an emergency rehab program.

The only Bangkok institution possibly as ubiquitous as the Buddhist temple is the distinctly more secular 7-Eleven chain of convenience stores. So numerous are its branches in central Bangkok that we like to challenge ourselves by finding a street corner from which we cannot glimpse two 7-Elevens within the same field of vision. Bangkok is home to over 1,300 of these florescent humanoid filling stations: Come here for toothpaste, cold beer, travel-sized shaving cream, Sangsom whiskey, *naam prik* chili paste, microwave pizza, fresh milk, fresh batteries or fresh condoms. Or just step in for a guaranteed blast of sub-zero air conditioning.

As indigenous as practically anything else in this city nowadays, these 24-hour shops are an integral part of non-stop Bangkok existence; people just seem to wander into them on instinct. Upon swinging through its glass door, each customer is personally greeted by counter staff with a corporate regulation chant of "*Sawatdii Kha!*" along with the trademark ding-dong chime of convenience stores worldwide (see "Ding Dong Addendum" on next page). With an average of 1,000 customers per day per branch, the "*Sawatdii Kha!*" greeting is uttered a whopping 474,500,000 times each year by 7-Eleven staff across the city. That's a lot of human energy that could have been spent on merit making (see "Tam Boon").

When you've got late-night munchies and feel like throwing every last bit of dietary caution to the wind, do this: Enter a 7-Eleven at around 3 AM, order a big juicy hot dog at the counter (some branches offer eight different varieties – bliss!) then proceed to the condiments stand. Stuff the bun with lettuce, tomatoes, cucumbers, mustard, ketchup and mayonnaise. Next – and this is the important part – grab a small bag of potato chips from the adjacent shelf and stuff as many chips as possible into the bun, creating a huge, crunchy, revolting mountain. Pay for everything at the cashier and try to look extremely proud of your creation. Ignore looks of disdain shot at you by the staff, for this act is an expression of your individuality, a way of boldly re-asserting your place in this world. They cannot be expected to understand.

Addendum: Operation Ding Dong

In a bold effort to investigate the supposed uniformity of 7-Eleven branches in Bangkok, we decided to check the famous shop doorbells, commonly known as "Ding Dongs." These are the chimes that come before the "*Sawatdii kha!*" when you step in and after the "See you next time" upon leaving.

Operation Ding Dong went like this: We secretly recorded the ding dong in a 7-Eleven shop on Sukhumvit Soi 71, then (wait for this) *crossed the road and recorded the ding dong at a rival 7-Eleven.* We then forwarded the ding dong audio samples to our dedicated *Bangkok Inside Out* Music Laboratory – the personal fiefdom of mad music scientist Dr. Stashek Maderovsky.

In a matter of hours Stashek got back to us with the shocking results: One ding dong was in C major and the other in E-flat major. He even furnished us with visual representations of the notes so that the world can see the difference:

In his formal report Stashek wrote: "I deplore the way people tend to think ding dongs are the same everywhere. It makes me so edgy. Particularly in Bangkok, where we're dealing with such a rich culture, obviously we're going to encounter numerous interesting layers, each different from the next. And I say, all of them have a right to exist side by side."

Stashek is currently under surveillance at Bumrungrad Hospital, where specialists are examining the numerous interesting layers inside his head in a bid to determine how they can possibly exist side by side.

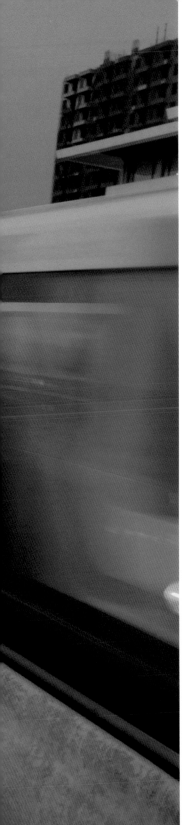

"Sataani toh pai Nana – Next station Nana,"* declares a confident Bangkok Transit System (BTS) operator over the PA system as the sky train glides smoothly into the spotless station. One could be forgiven for assuming it was always this simple to get around the city.

Back in the now-distant 1990s, traversing the city in a matter of minutes was a pipe dream for any Bangkokian who did not own a private helicopter. So hopeless was traffic that honoring an afternoon appointment across town meant leaving hours in advance, preferably armed with snacks, sandwiches, a portable potty, reading material and a prayer book. Salvation finally arrived in 1999 in the form of a 23km-long elevated train system, fully air-conditioned and completed a mere $900 million over budget.

The sky train changed not just travel time across the city, but the landscape itself. Commuters were suddenly able to view Bangkok's temples from above and *wai* them as their train passed overhead; parks were now visible, as was the city's ever-growing skyline. Owners of properties along the routes are thrilled, since their assets soared in value as soon as the new service began. Environmentalists aren't quite so impressed: They're scandalized by the unattractive steel and concrete structures, which trap bad air underneath and add sound pollution to an already noisy city.

Each day about 300,000 people ride the BTS's two lines, less than the predicted 430,000-passenger target. Many say it is because the fares – B10-40 per ride (about 25 cents to $1) – are too steep for low income commuters, who opt for a B4 bus ride. And many office workers commute from so far outside the city center that the sky train, even when combined with a free shuttle bus service, simply doesn't get them all the way home.

Inside the station, it's almost Singapore: no eating, drinking or smoking. If you step over the yellow line on the platform, the duty guard will shoot a horrified glance in your direction; his eyes scream scandal as he unleashes a deafening shriek from his whistle and everyone else looks on disapprovingly. *Don't* step over the yellow line.

Commuters once enjoyed quiet waits for the train, until the introduction of a boisterous PA system and large-screen TVs airing loud commercials. Bright adverts are splashed across the train carriages and product promotion posters decorate the insides. In fact, BTS stations have become shrines to commercialism, packed with newsagents, stalls selling 'Green Music', mobile phone vendors, bath product shops and teens distributing promotional leaflets for fast food.

Lazing about in temple courtyards, schmoozing on a hot afternoon by the doors of a 7-Eleven or snoozing under a noodle trolley in a *soi* (alley), dogs are an inseparable part of Bangkok's landscape. Sometimes it seems as if the municipality designated certain dogs to be responsible for specific parts of town. On Silom Road you'll notice that the dog idling near the entrance to the Thai Airways office behaves as if he's got a semi-official job there. In the future, perhaps we'll be able to email him or get him to check our Royal Orchid Plus mileage status.

Are soi dogs pretty? No they are not. Do they mostly have terrible skin, appear malnourished and suffer from near-complete hair loss? Mostly, they do. But that's part of their charm.

Life as a soi dog is all about being a zombie by day while waiting for night to fall. Many of the dogs we interviewed for this book noted that Bangkok Dog Elation Hours (or BDEH) are between about 1:22 AM and 3:57 AM, when they howl loudly, rule the city's backstreets with impunity, chat to each other and work on group issues. No wonder some pedestrians find it intimidating to roam Bangkok's alleyways during these sacred canine hours.

Like humans, some dogs make it to the very top of the society ladder. Thongdaeng, who was once a soi dog, became the king's favorite pet when she was rescued from the streets and brought to the Royal Palace as a puppy. The king eventually published a book about her, adorned with fine photos of lucky Thongdaeng and her puppies. The moral of the story? In Bangkok anyone can be a social climber.

Most of Thongdaeng's 300,000 friends still lay strewn in the city's polluted streets, contract multi-hued skin diseases and rely on food from kind-hearted residents. When nobody's around to feed them, like during the New Year holiday when the city is practically deserted, they can become quite aggressive. Tabloids love reporting messy incidents involving dogs and children and quite a bit of blood.

During the high-profile 2003 APEC summit, municipal authorities 'sanitized' the city by rounding up and transferring 3,000 dogs from central Bangkok to a huge pen near the Cambodian border. When it emerged there was insufficient food for them there, people sent personal donations to the starving, uprooted pooches – evidence that even in exile, soi dogs are regarded as real Bangkokians.

We're all familiar with those romanticized "Sights & Sounds Of…" TV spots reminding us that Karachi or Pyongyang are among 210 places we can watch a certain omnipresent cable news channel. But Bangkok is a city that truly lends itself to such exercises. Unlike other Asian metropolises that seem to drown in the din of their own traffic (Manila, anyone?) some unique and mostly wonderful sounds are an inseparable part of the Bangkok experience.

Surely the shrill, echoing blow of the boatman's whistle by the river taxi pier is part of life's soundtrack in this city. Watch the river vessel inch backward and forward to the fluctuating tones and musical patterns. Sense the rhythm. Now listen to the engines grind and roar into reverse, to the splash of water against the dock as the boat pulls in with that familiar thud, to the quick patter of feet as passengers hop on and off the deck. It's a Bangkok orchestra.

And what person who has been to a local kickboxing match (see "Muay Thai") can forget the mesmerizing wail of the traditional *phii chawa* (oboe) at the start of each bout? Or the warm Isaan melodies of *Luuk Thung* rising out from nearly every Bangkok taxi? Equally common, though less graceful, are the mushy beats of generic 'T-pop' heard in shopping malls across the city and the woefully off-key tones emanating from karaoke bars all over town.

In central Bangkok, blind musicians chant slow, haunting songs that crackle from a tenuously rigged amplifier, while coin-collecting helpers lead them patiently along bustling sidewalks. Overhead, a sky train whizzes by with a familiar swoosh, while the muted roar of a subway is just barely heard underfoot. At street level, food stall commotion provides its own distinctive soundtrack: deep fried locusts crackling in a wok; a hawker frantically pounding chili paste in a mortar; the noisy chatter of diners; and the mad clatter of dirty dishes being washed. This could only be Bangkok.

131

Like the dichotomy between experiences that are fun (see "Sanuk") and not fun (*mai sanuk*), culinary encounters in Bangkok can be divided into tasty – *aroi* – and not tasty – *mai aroi*.

When it comes to their cuisine, Bangkokians are fiercely opinionated and prone to declarations like "The noodles at this corner stall are *aroi*, but only when the vendor's wife makes them, not when the husband is there on his own. Too much fish sauce! *Mai aroi!*"

Even condiments can be an issue: An old auntie always seems to be on hand to insist we consume food items the 'correct way' – using *this* sauce or *this* spice with *this* dish, otherwise the whole thing will be, inevitably, *mai aroi*.

Quirks aside, Bangkok street food is one of the wonders of Asia, so much so that we often find ourselves planning a day's schedule and route according to food stalls we wish to raid in different corners of the city (yes – we are *that* busy).

"From Chinatown to Silom to Khaosan Road," writes Rachada Rithdee in *Sawasdee* magazine, "vendor's stalls enliven the capital's busy thoroughfares…Cheap, quick and unceremonious, sidewalk eateries speak the spirit of Bangkok the same way as do smoky cafés for Paris or rowdy pubs for London. Look closely: Street eating represents the most democratic form of indulgence, as chauffeured millionaires sit alongside laborers and super-hip yuppies mingle with factory workers. Dashing club-goers step in for a bowl of noodles before heading off for a wild night on glitzy Sukhumvit, while night watchmen just off the graveyard shift elbow them aside for their late supper. Taste is usually a great social divider, but irresistible Bangkok street food brings everyone down to the same level."

Timing is key in the Bangkok food stall world: Some culinary venues are early morning affairs; others specialize in mid-day cuisine, and many are strictly nocturnal. Show up at a night stall in the morning and you might just encounter an office supplies shop – the owner grinning at you with a mix of sympathy and ridicule. And if you routinely wake up at 9 AM, you'll never meet the plump woman who each morning sells fried Chinese doughnuts and soy milk to your neighbors. At 8:59 she'll vanish, leaving behind just two big oil stains on the sidewalk, to be quickly concealed by the fruit seller who arrives at approximately 9:02.

TABLOIDS

สำนักพิมพ์ออนไลน์

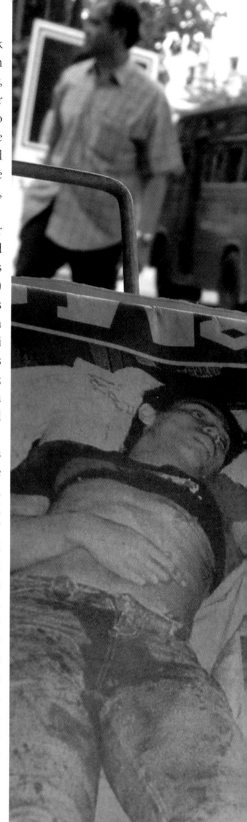

A prerequisite for the screaming front page of any Bangkok tabloid is that it feature at least one photo of a crime victim animatedly pointing his or her finger at an alleged perpetrator, usually with police officers standing by. Whether or not other suspects are still at large or whether the suspect in the photo has even been charged is immaterial. The pointing gesture says it all. Staged pictures are a huge part of what defines local tabloids, and one of our obscure Bangkok pastimes (we have many) is scouring newsstands for just such dramatic images, usually while waiting for the bus.

A tabloid's front page is normally cluttered with eight or so stories, all of which inevitably continue on page 15. And what *really* makes a Bangkok tabloid editor drool over his keyboard? Any photo of a handcuffed *farang* (foreigner) caught at Don Muang Airport with 1,250 ecstasy pills in his shampoo bottle (or even better, up his butt); A *farang* (a different one, presumably) decked out in a traditional Thai costume after marrying a Thai soap opera celebrity; bodies of any kind, the gory parts censored by blurred rectangles; reports of lottery hysteria; a sex scandal involving a government official; and, of course, a few football-related stories.

Thai Rath (nicknamed *Hua Kiew*, or 'green head', for its logo) is the mother of Thai tabloids and controls 60% of the market. Next in line is *Daily News* (known as *Hua Baan Yen*, or 'fuchsia head'). Both are considered *chao baan*, or 'villager', newspapers and focus on soft news as opposed to 'quality' papers like *Matichon*, which are identified with the educated middle class. Bangkokians love their newspapers: Circulation in Bangkok accounts for 50% of sales countrywide, and this is reflected in the number of stories covered from the capital.

The dream of one day choosing the winning lottery numbers (see "Lottery") is a national obsession, and *Thai Rath* is famous for planting hints on its horoscope page suggesting possible magic numbers. Synopses of upcoming soap opera episodes are also hot ("Manit discovers Tarnthip is dating Nithi, the son of the company president, and tells Namfon about it; Saichon dies in a car accident in Pattaya"). Tabloids are devoured from cover to cover at just about every streetside noodle shop across the country, hence the soup stains.

รวบทันควั
มือวางเพ

◀ **เหยื่อทมิฬ** นายประดิษฐ์ สุภา-
มูล ถูกนายอนันต์ แสงบุญ เลขานายก
อบต.ร้องวัวแดง อ.สันกำแพง จ.เชียง-
ใหม่ รุมยำก่อนยิงตายพร้อมนายนรินทร์
ธรรมกาศ (ภาพเล็ก) กับเพื่อนอีกศพ
รวม 3 ศพ เหตุเพราะเข้าใจผิดที่เหยื่อ
โวยร้านคาราโอเกะปิดบริการเร็ว.

แฝงเป็นคร
สอนศาสน
กับศิษย์
ทหาร

TAM BOON

ทำบุญ

Take an early morning stroll through any Bangkok neighborhood and you'll likely hear a quiet patter of feet shuffling along the road. Suddenly, Buddhist monks appear from around the corner, hands clasping begging bowls, heads pointed humbly downward toward the pavement, part of the daily alms collecting ritual. It's a classic Bangkok scene, the stuff not just of ancient custom or shiny postcards, but of everyday life in this city.

Nearly all Thai Buddhists engage in some form of *tam boon* (merit making). *Tam boon* means to do something good for society or nature, and is thought to bring rewards in the next life or, conversely, to ward off bad karma. There are infinite ways to *tam boon*: releasing animals such as turtles, birds and fish back into nature; offering alms to monks on their early morning rounds; making a donation at the temple or volunteering in the community. The *when* is often as important as the *what*. Many Thais choose to make merit on their birthday, upon graduation, or on other auspicious dates.

One recent poll found that 97% of Bangkokians believed giving alms to monks each New Year's Day would ensure they encountered only good things in life. Liberating cows destined for slaughter came in second, with 85% of respondents citing it as a huge source of merit. Turtle release was next at 74%, but the big surprise was birds: 61% of respondents felt freeing birds just didn't do the trick.

Tam boon can also serve as a plea for forgiveness. During the 2004 bird flu crisis, the Ministry of Agriculture organized a *tam boon* ceremony in Bangkok "to ease public guilt" over the 26 million chickens slaughtered to halt the spread of the disease, and to bless the dead chickens' spirits. 108 monks in yellow robes chanted blessings for the dearly departed birds before senior officials served participants a meal of…fried chicken and chicken curry.

Chaowalate Jarubun, who worked as an executioner for twenty years at Bangkok's maximum security Bang Kwang prison, might have pushed the notion of *tam boon* a bit too far. "After executions, I would go to the temple to make merit for the dead, to be sure there was nothing between their spirit and mine," he told newspapers in 2004 – the same year Thailand switched from death by firing squad to lethal injection.

TAXIS & HELP RADIO

Bangkok taxi drivers do not carry change. Ever. And if you ask them to slow down, they will turn to you and laugh. A nice, good hearted laugh, not a mean one. Another neat thing is that zero training is required to become a taxi driver in Bangkok. That's right, anybody can show up, grab a taxi license from the Traffic Department, buy a used chauffeur shirt, rent a taxi for twelve hours and the rest is history (or, alas, reality).

A majority of the city's 100,000 drivers come from Isaan (see "Chao Isaan"), share a rented room with friends, work 12-hour shifts and miss home terribly. They'll normally pull in at least B1,200 (around $40), but they spend B550 on vehicle lease and B500 on fuel, hence their love for non-metered fares and their persistent denial of the existence of Thai coins.

It's never hard to hail a cab in Bangkok because of an estimated 30% oversupply rate. With the late-1990s economic crisis, the allowable shelf life for taxis was raised from 8 to 12 years, so today many of these older taxis are in a horrendous shape, smell awful and, with a broken air-conditioner, keep about as cool as a Dhaka rickshaw in June. But the drivers are friendly and their tape decks invariably churn out soothing *Luuk Thuung* music – a reminder of the exotic, multi-cultural life we all lead here in Thailand.

Rather than following an organized religion, Bangkok cabbies become fiercely loyal members of a radio station. The most famous is *Jo So Roi*. It started as a community station in 1991 and was the first to provide Bangkokians with badly needed 24-hour traffic reports. It was an instant hit with thousands of listeners, many of whom were taxi drivers. Only registered members are allowed to report on the sacred topic of traffic patterns or offer navigation tips of their own.

Before long *Jo So Roi* found itself dealing with other city issues, like assistance to flood victims, locating lost wallets in long gone taxis, or bailing out a fellow driver stuck headlight-high on Wireless Road during a monsoon downpour . The station's popularity begged competition, and new stations like *So Wo Po Kaosib Ed* and *Ruam Duay Chuay Kan* soon hit the airwaves. Today nearly every Bangkok taxi driver belongs to a favorite help radio station, and wouldn't listen to any other.

For many Bangkokians, Thonburi, the mostly residential half of the city across the Chao Phraya River, is the Great Unknown, or simply the Other Side. Its fifteen minutes of fame came in the form of fifteen years of reign. In 1767, after the fall of Ayutthaya, King Taksin made it the Siamese capital until the current Chakri dynasty moved the whole governance business across the river in 1782. Thonburi is still home to a number of famous sites such as Wat Arun and the Royal Barges Museum, but otherwise it's a rather nondescript, forgotten place.

Many Bangkok office workers live in *Fang Thon* ("Thonburi side") and commute each day to work. And if you're a Peace Corps volunteer, language student or PhD researcher, you'll probably want to make your home in Thonburi. It's far cheaper than Bangkok proper, and a Thonburi address guarantees truckloads of street cred in the 'going native' sense ("Yeah, I've heard of Sukhumvit," you'll say smugly, "but I'm actually living over in Thonburi, where the streets have no names and my next door neighbor sells fresh jackfruit and Laotian tiger balm from the back of a canoe…")

Thonburi certainly has its charms. Linked to Bangkok by twelve bridges and countless two-baht shuttle barges, it's a relaxed, distinctly low-rise place. It boasts terrific waterways, a small floating market and some huge shopping centers intended to keep at least a modest share of Bangkok's frenzied consumer consumption on the west side of the river. Some luxury apartments and international hotel chains have erected properties on the Thonburi side of the Chao Phraya, securing fantastic waterfront views at an affordable cost.

Undoubtedly one of the most relaxing, memorable Bangkok experiences is a trip through Thonburi's elaborate network of *khlong* (see "Khlong") on a *reua hang yao* (long tail boat), which allows a close-up look at the unhurried life along the city's suburban waterways.

143

Foreigners strolling through Bangkok can expect a barrage of catcalls shouted at them by people offering a curious slew of services. At the airport it's "Hotel, Sir?" and in Patpong at night it's "Sex show?" "Body massage for you?" and "Sexy movie?" Along Sukhumvit Road, Sikh tailors stand outside their shops beckoning "Sir, do come in for a quick look!"

Far more sophisticated are Bangkok's shameless gem scam touts. Want to experience the saga in person? Stand in the vicinity of the Grand Palace holding up a fully extended map of Bangkok; wear a pair of baggy Bermuda shorts that expose your white, hairy legs or your recently acquired Ko Samui sunburn; sweat profusely and squint hard at the map; appear utterly confused, but also friendly, curious, trusting and inherently optimistic. You shall be approached in a matter of seconds.

A *tuk tuk* driver with remarkably good English will pull over to inform you that, alas, "Wat Phra Kaew is closed for a Buddhist holiday, but I'll take you to a better place," suggesting an hour-long tour around town for B10 (25 cents) and mentioning that today is the final day of an annual duty free gem sale. You hop in and say nothing.

You're taken to another temple, where you encounter another friendly Thai fellow who coincidentally asks whether you've heard about the Gem Promotion. Turns out he paid for his lavish honeymoon in Sydney by selling gems he bought right around the corner. Next stop is the gem shop. Honest drivers will admit they receive gasoline vouchers for every tourist they land at a shop, and in their sweet Thai way will ask you to simply show your face inside "And then we go – no problem!" Inside, you'll likely be handed a chilled drink and 'taught' to differentiate between real gems and fakes.

Now that you're an expert, you'll likely end up buying gems that are worth about 5% of what you paid. Some tourists aren't even *that* lucky: their cold beverage was drugged and they wake up on the street an hour later with credit card receipts for thousands of dollars of gems they just purchased, minus the gems…

Precious stones are part of Thailand's exotic image, so when gem scams began featuring a bit too prominently in the tourist 'experience' in the 1990s, the Thai Tourist Police launched a vigorous and quite successful 'Just Say No' campaign.

The average travel time between home and office in Bangkok is 96 minutes. The average car speed during rush hour in the City of Angels is 25km per hour. No wonder cars here look like homes on wheels, furnished with snacks, newspapers, Game Boys, pillows, water bottles and… 'Comfort 100' – the mobile potty for men.

Traffic remains notorious despite the sky train and new subway system because the number of new cars in Bangkok increases 10% each year while road space grows only 1.5%. For many Bangkokians, a car is a status symbol, proof that they've 'made it' (whereas using public transportation would suggest they hadn't.) Moreover, park-and-ride facilities are rare, making it difficult for suburban commuters to leave their vehicles at sky train or subway stations before heading into town.

To date, there has been no serious municipal campaign encouraging residents to use public transportation. One distinguished lady we know had another explanation for not using public transport: If she had to run up and down sky train station stairs and then hop a motorcycle taxi in Bangkok's humid, polluted air, she'd reach her office looking like a mop. This, we thought, would actually be quite funny.

The worst cases of *rot tid* (traffic jams) are typically right before and after Songkran, the Thai Lunar New Year holiday. In Songkran 1995, for example, drivers going to and from Don Muang airport spent up to eight grueling hours in traffic, and some actually opted to walk 30km in the April heat. Many flights were delayed, as neither passengers nor crew could make it to the terminal in time. Motorcycle taxi drivers (see "Motosai") made out like bandits that day, shuttling agitated, suitcase-wielding passengers from traffic jam to airport and helping them with dramatic last-minute entries to the departure hall.

Tip: If you want to make someone's life really miserable, tell them they absolutely *must* go sightseeing around Bangkok's unique Kaset intersection in the north of the city, preferably before sunset, at around 5:30 PM. It's the city's most congested junction during rush hour, and drivers routinely spend thirty minutes to an hour stuck

UNIFORMS

เครื่องแบบ

As uniform festishists, walking in Bangkok has never been easy for us (don't ask – it's not what you think). Everyone in this city seems to sport his or her own uniform – university students, teachers, civil servants, department store sales staff, bus conductors, masseuses, security patrolmen and sometimes even sex workers. Outfits provide a sense of belonging as well as evidence to friends and neighbors that the wearer holds a steady job. Uniforms also represent a huge industry in Thailand, to the tune of about $100 million in annual revenues.

Thais wear uniforms from a young age: Children in Bangkok are often decked out in distinguished kindergarten uniforms when they're three or four years old. From then on, they'll normally don uniforms until they are in their twenties – yes, the petite young girls in Siam Square wearing black skirts and white shirts are *not* in junior high school, but university.

Apparently, the snug brown outfits worn by Thailand's policemen are a turn-on for an alarming number of people. According to newspaper reports, an average of four hundred complaints are filed each month by cops who receive obscene calls from admirers, mainly women and gay men. Fans even maintain a website dedicated to the figure-hugging attire: www.misterpolice.com.

Uniforms can occasionally serve as icebreakers, especially when they bear nametags. We'll sometimes approach a military officer on a public boat ride along the Chao Phraya River and ask the poor guy, "So…*Khun Somchai*! How are things in the navy?"

The definition of uniform can stretch (no pun intended) to other accessories. Our friend Pam, a flight attendant for Thai Airways, moans about having to carry around her black company-issued suitcase even when there is nothing in it, solely because it's part of the uniform. A resigned Pam smiles sadly to herself each time she lugs the empty thing to her mom's car after a quickie to Chiang Rai.

For some, uniforms are a matter of life and death. Rowdy students, usually from technical schools, are notorious for bashing pupils wearing outfits of rival schools and collecting the victim's buckle, which bears the school emblem. Clever kids wishing to avoid getting clobbered leave home in nondescript 'civilian' clothing and change into uniform once they're near or inside their school. This has sparked an innovative, quite prosperous new industry: Shops adjacent to school compounds now provide locker rental to 148 uniform-wary students.

It ranks as one of Bangkok's quirkiest spectacles. You're enjoying a roadside Singha beer when suddenly an enormous, visibly downtrodden Dumbo appears from around the corner, lumbering casually down a street of night clubs and modern office buildings as if contemplating whether to window shop or meet his mates for happy hour at the Hard Rock Café. It's a scene so bizarre even Haruki Murakami, master of outlandish (and normally fictitious) scenarios, included it in a short story.

Making money from elephants is no easy tusk. Laboring in fields or forests, they usually bring in just B60 (around $1.50) a day. But mahouts can generate B800 (about $20) a day from urban begging, since many Thais view elephant feeding as a form of merit making (see "Tam Boon"), and extra cash comes from charging tourists for snapshots. Roaming through Bangkok with an elephant is illegal, but many owners risk it, head for the big city and schlep their helpless friend through traffic and pollution all evening. Some mahouts even pump their elephants with amphetamines so they can roam 24/7. Streetwalking elephants often have a shiny CD (blank, we're assuming) hanging from their tail as a makeshift light reflector.

Urban elephants are symptomatic of a wider problem in the region. Logging has meant ever-shrinking forests, fewer elephant job opportunities, shorter food supplies and therefore elephants and owners struggling for survival in their traditional environment. Around two hundred elephants regularly roam the streets of Bangkok and authorities say at least half were smuggled into the country from Burma and Cambodia (*That* explains it: On various occasions we tried communicating with them in Thai, but zilch, yok, nada, rien!). A new municipal squad is supposed to round them up and move them to safe havens outside of town, where they are slated to become government employees (not too shabby!) and help forestry staff patrol protected woodlands. Their mahouts will get them back only if they can prove rightful ownership and produce work permits.

During preparations for the 2004 International AIDS Conference in Bangkok, controversy erupted over the event's logo. Thai community groups proposed an image of two elephants having sex, but health authorities criticized the suggested emblem because the bull wasn't wearing a condom while going at it. The chosen logo wasn't nearly as arousing. It depicted three elephants simply standing in a row.

URBAN ELEPHANTS

ช้างเร่ร่อนในเมือง

151

WHISKEY, COKE & ICE

วิสกี้ โคก น้ำแข็ง

The art of sharing cheap Thai whiskey at a loud Bangkok pub has all the ritualistic fidgeting of an elaborate Japanese tea ceremony, but little of the elegance or flair. Still, it's an endearing practice.

At a table of friends, the *nong* (literally 'younger sibling,' but really anyone more junior in age) serves the *phii*, or 'older sibling'. Armed with a pair of tongs, the *nong* will patiently pluck ice from a bucket at the end of the table, drop it into a glass, add the whiskey and stir in some Coke. Finally, he or she will serve it politely to the 'elder' friend, who might be all of eight months their senior. Once the glass is empty, the *nong* will dutifully refill it. It's not so much about subservience as it is a friendly, traditional form of respect. After all, every *nong*, depending on the age of others at a particular gathering, will at some point be somebody's *phii*.

The ritual isn't just in the serving, however. Whiskey – usually a cheap, local variety like Sangsom or Mekong rather than imported brands like Black Label or Chivas – is the beverage of choice at most middle-class Thai gatherings. Regulars will often buy and keep their own big bottle of whiskey at a favorite bar. The bottle will be labeled with their name, stored safely on a shelf and pulled out any time they show up. Whiskey is typically downed with a mixer (usually Coke or soda water) rather than straight, and accompanied by an assortment of spicy bar snacks. This allows the alcohol to seep in slowly so that revelers can spend hours enjoying live music or karaoke until emerging from the bar pissed out of their minds.

On holidays, particularly the Thai New Year, *Songkran*, excessive drinking always means a serious increase in road accidents. The government runs campaigns against drunk drinking, usually to little avail. Offenders are hit with fines and sometimes made to sweep roads as a form of community service. When celebrity heartthrob Willy McIntosh (see "Luuk Kreung") was caught driving under the influence in 2004, he was fined B4,000 (around $100) and had to distribute stickers to drivers while wearing a jacket that read 'No Drunk Driving'. Said the judge: "Having Willy sweep roads would have only caused traffic jams."

YAA BAA

เยาบ้า

Bangkokians from nearly all walks of life have discovered the rapidly spreading social poison known as *Yaa Baa*, or 'crazy medicine'. Slum dwellers, taxi drivers, sailors, construction workers, novice monks, students and clubbers are among those who've grown desperately addicted to the popular, easy-to-make methamphetamine fix. Thailand's Ministry of Health recently estimated that over 4% of the country's 63-million people are addicted to drugs, especially methamphetamines.

Yaa Baa is produced mainly in neighboring Myanmar, but lately manufacturing has even found its way to the outskirts of Bangkok. The narcotic, which floods the user's brain with dopamine, sharpens the senses and induces a feeling of invincibility and euphoria, hence its nickname, 'the happiness drug'.

In 2002 the government vowed to eradicate the narcotics trade. Raids, shootings, arrests, even extra-judicial killings ensued, but none of this has killed off the industry, and *Yaa Baa* remains the most popular vice in Bangkok. The Khlong Toey super-slum (see "Khlong Toey") is the drug's main trading ground.

One obstacle in combating the drug is its clean, slick image and user-friendliness. The pill looks modern and fun, and with manufacturing instructions readily available on the internet it's almost as easy to make as it is to take; *Yaa Baa* comes in as many as ninety different forms, and can be dissolved in a glass of water, taken intravenously, pulverized, inhaled, or even smoked. The vice is also affordable: In some parts of town it sells for as little as B80 (around $2) a pill – much cheaper than other drugs.

Drug trafficking in Thailand carries the death penalty but plenty of people still risk it, and the list of hiding places for their pills reads like a *Where's Waldo* of the narcotics world: in large oil drums; in a condom inside the body of a female tourist; in a military truck parked at an east Bangkok shopping mall; in custom-built hidden chambers above the wheels of a pickup truck; in a forest in the Mae Sot district; in a cigarette carton; and, ingeniously, in a plain paper bag.

ยมพบกับ

รมแฟชั่นไทย

งาดเวทีโลก

My
Grace Hotel
Weekend

by Daniel Ziv

For years I had watched them shuffle up and down the sloped driveway. Burly, bearded men, hands sometimes interlocked, eyes usually staring down at the pavement. When their leather sandals disappeared beneath the long white cotton of their robes, it seemed as though they were gliding up and down that driveway like desert sheikhs or tribal nomads entering and departing a mysterious urban oasis. It's an exoticized image, no doubt, but the Grace Hotel – a Bangkok institution in the heart of the city's tiny Arab enclave of Nana – is indeed an unusual place. Truth be told, it's got a pretty seedy reputation. It lies in close proximity to one of the city's main prostitution districts and is known as a post-2AM partying venue for the drunken, stoned and desperate. So for every few white cotton robes descending that driveway, you'll normally spot a mock-leather miniskirt a few sizes too small. But rather than continuing to imagine it from the outside, I decided to check myself in for the weekend.

A week before my stay the telephone reservation is brief and efficient. The hotel is already booked to 85% capacity but I'm still able to choose from three classes of rooms in the Grace's two wings, the prices ranging from B700-1,000 (around $18 to $25) per night. I choose something mid-budget. The following Friday afternoon I ascend that same busy driveway, enter through the glass doors and proceed to the reception desk.

The lobby is a flurry of activity, so much so that I can hardly stay focused on my check-in form. Everyone in sight appears to be of Middle Eastern origin and as a Caucasian guest I am shot a somewhat bemused first glance by the young check-in clerk, though she proves friendly and helpful. Travelers keep pouring out of taxis, piling luggage trolleys high and congregating noisily around sofas, coffee tables and elevators. Some of the more distinguished Middle Eastern guests (this I gather by the quality of their robes and size of their girths) have arrived with a substantial private entourage – family, friends and business associates – parking themselves over entire sections of the vast lobby, kicking back like weary Bahraini oil barons at a Manama country club. It's an unlikely mix of patrons: About half appear to be single men who've come to the Grace to release some pent-up sexual energy while the other half are families – big, busy ones – on some form of city holiday.

If one thing distinguishes the Grace's interior it's the unbelievable number of signs, placards and notices hung all over the premises. Or perhaps it just seems like a lot because every sign is repeated in Arabic – from the 'No Smoking' warnings to the restaurant promotion posters and the board advertising floating market tours at the interestingly-named Disco Travel agency by the main entrance. Everywhere I turn there is so much to read. It starts to feel like homework.

My first real surprise comes when the bellhop shows me the room. At B800 per night I had prepared for a claustrophobic weekend in a dark, grimy room. In fact, I was almost hoping for this because a squalid, decaying space would have sounded a whole lot funkier. Alas, the room is spacious, bright, airy and exceptionally clean. There's a writing desk and mini bar and satellite TV with eight different Arabic-language channels. There's even a view of the surrounding cityscape. The bathroom boasts a full tub, hot water and a high-pressure shower, and, crucially, enough floor space in front of the toilet to spread out the latest issues of *Farang* magazine, *The Nation* and the Arabian Cuisine section of the room service menu. This, is far as I'm concerned is living it up. I'm happy.

The hotel didn't forget to scatter a dozen more notices and brochures in the room (whoever scored the card-production contract for the Grace is doing solid business). A desktop promo card advertises "Touch and Taste: The new origination new style of classic pizza." Next to it, another card advising of charges levied "in case if you're likely to obtain for souvenir or perhaps some damaged," includes "Sink: B2,000" and "Cigarette burnt on bed cover: B3,000-5,000." I decide immediately that I won't obtain the sink for souvenir. No siree. Not at that price.

The elevator offers no respite from the relentless sign assault: Here, a glass-framed poster advertising the hotel's '24-Hour Turkish Spa & Massage' depicts towel-clad Caucasian women laying luxuriously on a massage bed, surrounded by flower petals, plants and aromatic oils. I descend the dimly-lit spiral staircase to the spa on the basement floor, where there are, of course, no towel-clad Caucasian women, flower petals or aromatic oils. Instead, an ebullient *mamasan* in bright red lipstick and badly smudged mascara escorts me to a huge glass display window. Behind it sit a few dozen women who are dressed – most just barely – in an assortment of garish outfits.

They are all staring upward at what must be a TV set above the glass, but when alerted to my presence huddle quickly together, fiddle nervously with their hair pins and bra straps, giggle amongst themselves a bit and broadcast manufactured smiles towards the glass panel. It's a typical Bangkok 'Turkish Sauna' – a buzzword for a fishbowl where women are numbers and customers choose between chubby and petite, old and young, 'good massage' or just 'good time, massage not so good.' The lipsticked *mamasan* shows me the massage rooms, Regular and VIP, the latter more spacious and luxurious and furnished with a full-sized Jacuzzi. All rooms come with fluffy towels, a bottle of baby oil and an inflatable mattress on which Bangkok's infamous soapy body massage is performed. For all the tantalizing amenities it's a downright depressing place, resembling a cold, sterile hospital ward more than any kind of cozy or erotic love nest. The *mamasan* urges me to choose one of her fine ladies for a two-hour, B2,000 'all-inclusive' soapy body massage. I decline, and offer *her* a soapy body massage for B3,000. She's not particularly amused. I internalize the rejection and head back upstairs.

I use the other elevator this time – opportunity to enjoy a *different* promotional poster, this one inquiring: "Did you remember of your last dinner, it's good taste or not?" I couldn't quite recall my last dinner and figured this was a signal to head straight back down to the Grace's restaurant and learn what memorable dinners are all about. The restaurant is dimly lit and a bit drab, but my window seat overlooks the Grace's driveway, a strategic view that allows me to watch the comings and goings and human interaction by the hotel entrance. I'm served a hearty platter of lamb kebab, hummus, *moutabel*, pita bread and pickles. It is indeed a "good taste" – to quote that elevator ad – and at B200 (about $5) for the whole meal, it is also good value.

It's 9 PM and there's a whole lot of noise outside my room. It's mostly women chattering in Arabic, scurrying back and forth between rooms along our corridor and making – for want of a better term – 'arrangements' of some sort. I'm not sure what it is they constantly need to arrange. Sometimes they have children in tow; occasionally they move bags or shoes or food containers from one guest room to the next; or else they just knock on a door, convey some information and leave. What a hectic holiday.

I head out for a stroll. I've been here barely twenty-four hours and already I'm becoming addicted to chicken and beef shawarma. There's a stall right around the corner from the Grace and it serves the succulent meat wraps for B50. My problem is that the shawarma are small enough so that psychologically I can write them off as a snack rather than a meal. The vendor here already knows me. He's a friendly guy but it's a worrying dynamic. I stuff my face, drip *tahina* sauce all over my shirt and return to the Grace.

The hotel's signature late-night entertainment is *Arabian Nights*, a belly-dancing extravaganza staged in the dark, palatial nightclub adjacent to the lobby. The doorman, a middle-aged Thai gentleman in a shiny blue-striped suit, collects my cover charge, winks and promises I'll love the show. "It is very special, the best dancing in Bangkok. I hope you will enjoy our ladies." It's 1 AM and the place is still pretty empty, so I return to the entrance. "Um, when do things start happening?" I ask the blue striped suit. "Not before 2 o'clock. Maybe better you go for walk and come back later." I can't believe it's 1:15 and I'm too *early* for something, but I head out to Nana

once again, bypass the shawarma stall because the remaining meat appears sad and tired now, and stroll through Nana's back alleys listening to *Al-Jazeera* pretty much by osmosis.

The blue-striped suit greets me with his trademark wink and grin when I return at 1:53. I step inside. The place is pretty packed now, a friendly mix of men and women, nearly all Middle Eastern and quite elegantly dressed. Most of the seating is arranged around large nightclub tables or clusters of VIP sofas next to the stage and dance floor, but I find one of the last remaining seats on a long plush sofa against the wall, next to some college-aged Middle Eastern boys and their Thai girlfriends. One of the girlfriends smiles at me, says hello and shows me the bleeping lights on her sticker-adorned mobile phone. I express my admiration for the special effects and decline a gracious offer to be introduced over the phone to her friend, even though this friend is, reportedly, "very beautiful, I think she like you very much mister." The show is about to start, and I will tolerate no such distractions.

The lights dim. The soulful notes of an Arabic *oud* pierce the silence, followed by a hollow, infectious drumbeat that quickly assumes control of the room. The audience responds enthusiastically, mimicking the drumbeat with sharp, steady claps. They shift rhythmically in their seats, breaking into knowing smiles before a spotlight suddenly illuminates the live band on stage. The band is good. *Very* good. And when the belly dancer appears from behind the stage curtain, the clapping grows louder and the smiles broader, accompanied now by spirited whoops. The dancer – Lebanese, I'm told – is beautiful and blonde and voluptuous and her belly begins doing impossible things. Soon she descends from the stage and proceeds straight into the eager crowd. Patrons approach her in turn, pulling wads of banknotes from their pockets and showering the belly queen with paper baht. A club attendant quickly gathers the money from the carpet and whisks it to safety behind the stage. The belly dancer picks up her pace now and the bells around her ankles and wrists are jiggling as wildly as her mountainous breasts. The money showers continue, the whoops grow louder, more patrons take to the dance floor now, and it's a happy, happy place. A few hours of this exotica is about all I can take. The blue-striped suit allows me to exit

after I assure him that I loved the show and would be returning in the not-too-distant future with some of my friends.

The corner where the Grace's driveway meets the end of Soi Nana has lots on offer besides kebabs. Stalls selling fresh lychee, pomelo and rambutan sit alongside stands hawking crispy fried cockroaches and beetles, the latter a perennial favorite of the young Isaan girls who ply Nana's streets each night. There are even vendors selling remote-control airplanes. I can't think of any reason to acquire a remote-control airplane at this particular juncture of my life but the lychee are plump and delicious and I spend the next thirty minutes devouring a kilo of them out of a plastic bag like roasted peanuts.

Nearby, I wander up to an outdoor bar crowded with a dozen or so African patrons, all of whom, it turns out, are Congolese, and all of whom are lip-synching the words and tapping by their feet to the urgent beat of Central African music. I share a beer with William, from Kinshasa, here on business for the fifth time this year. He imports apparel to the DRC and hardly ever moves from this particular bar when in town to place clothing orders. "This is where my friends hang out," he tells me, "and this is the only music I like. It's the best music. Congolese." He breaks into a huge grin, throws his head back and laughs uncontrollably. "My fifth beer!" he howls.

The next night I decide to sample an unconventional hotel facility. The four-lane bowling alley in the Grace's lobby is undoubtedly one of the coolest features in an already very colorful place. It's lodged between the restaurant and nightclub, where in most hotels you'd find the beauty salon or flower shop or newsstand, and it's open all night. At midnight I step in and pay B150 to bowl a few frames. Shoe rental costs extra but is still very reasonably priced, I decide, for a four-lane late-night hotel bowling alley in the heart of major Southeast Asian capital. My first game is mediocre and I can't decide what's more pathetic, my 93 score or the fact that I'm standing here alone on a Saturday night at 12:17AM in jeans and bowling shoes actually agonizing over a gutter shot.

I begin reflecting on what all of this might say about my life when, luckily, I am interrupted Yasin – a slim, mustached, jovial fellow from Kuwait. He has apparently been watching my game – hence the pained grimace he wears on

his face now – and applauds loudly when I manage a spare in my last frame. I invite him to play the next game with me and he obliges. Yasin is in his mid-forties, a businessman who comes to Bangkok every few months "for business and pleasure" and trades in textiles between Asia and the Middle East. We aren't very far into the small talk when he throws his first ball, which, to my uncharitable dismay, is a clean strike. Yasin skips back over to me wearing a childish grin and slaps my sweaty palm with a loud high-five. "That was amazing!" I offer. "Yes, I like to play bowling" he confesses, "and sometimes I can do five or six of those in a row..." *Fuck,* I think to myself while doing some quick calculations in my head, *this casual joker is borderline professional.* Ten minutes and five Yasin strikes later, he has 276 points to my 71 and I'm feeling significantly worse than before. He's a good sport about it, though, offering cheers and back slaps each time my ball knocks over a measly three or four pins.

I swallow my pride and remind myself: *You're here to work on a book. Don't feel wounded. Don't let Yasin's friendly support humiliate you further. He's a great bowler, yes. He probably trains for days in between business trips at one of the swankiest alleys in Kuwait City. He's probably one of those guys who owns a world-class custom-designed bowling ball, with matching leather case. He probably has a personal coach and absolutely no life outside of bowling. A life of strikes and more strikes and the occasional spare. His fingers are surely bent and callused. What a meek, miserable man.*

I'm already feeling sorry for Yasin and his pitiful bowler's life when he releases the final ball of the game – a fucking strike – and walks over graciously to shake my hand. *Fucker.*

"Now, we take drinks at the disco downstairs," he announces matter-of-factly. "I want to show you some women." He scoops up our bowling shoes and returns them to the cashier, then leads me through the lobby, down the staircase and into the dark, loud, vibrating place he describes as his "favorite place in the whole city."

The Grace Hotel Disco is considered Bangkok's meat market of last resort due to its late operating hours and the girls who 'work' there – essentially unwanted leftovers from establishments that shut their doors a few hours earlier. These women rank pretty close to the bottom of Bangkok's nocturnal food chain: Winding up at the Grace Disco at 4 AM means

business *really* hasn't been going well.

I quickly conclude that Yasin must be sympathetic towards underdogs: He seems to know half the girls in the club on a first-name basis and proceeds to introduce me to a dozen plump, giggly friends decked out in plastic micro-minis and translucent tops that leave little to the imagination. He orders us some drinks but disappears onto the dance floor after a few sips. I soon spot him: He is in the center of a six-woman circle, hairy arms outstretched toward the heavens, gold chain swinging wildly around his neck, mustache framing an ecstatic smile that seems to say "I *may* just get lucky *six* times tonight, but first, I'm gonna dance like I mean it!"

Just when it feels like things are about to get down and dirty the music fades, the lights come on and an announcer invites a guest performer to the stage to mark the Euro Cup final that will be played later tonight. The performer is a ten-year-old boy wearing a shiny football jersey, cleated shoes and a cocky grin. Thumping background music comes on and the tiny kid hops on the stage and, like an Energizer bunny on ecstasy, launches into a frantic display of dazzling soccer technique: He bounces a ball off his feet, knees and head for over seven minutes without letting it touch the floor once. The audience cheers louder with every passing minute. You'd think it was the buxom belly dancer we were gawking at.

Finally, the ball drops to the floor, to a collective and very sympathetic sigh from the crowd. The boy has done us proud, is the overall sentiment, and a handful of generous patrons run up and place a few bills into the kid's shiny sports bag. The lights dim once again, the plump prostitutes return to the dance floor and the disco returns to its naughty, gyrating self.

I exit to the lounge just outside the disco and walk over to the gift shop. It sell just about everything a young working woman could ever need for an overnight gig at the Grace: toothbrushes and toothpaste, breath mints, miniature packs of Pringles, assorted chocolate bars and teddy bears in all sizes, some emblazoned with the words "I Love You" on the chest. Ah, romance.

RECOMMENDED ENGLISH-LANGUAGE PUBLICATIONS ON BANGKOK

1. *Time Out Bangkok* (**Penguin Travel, B695**) is far and away the best general guidebook to Bangkok. We're amazed at everything editor Philip Cornwel-Smith and his team managed to cram into this compact volume, and particularly impressed by the many boxed features on everything from the local art and music scene to street carts, meditation, and child labor. The listings in here are the most comprehensive and switched-on we've seen, and the edgy photography is refreshing. This is the real deal.

2. *Bangkok* by **William Warren** (**Talisman, B695**) is a delightful account of the city's history, modern-day growing pains and human energy. Warren writes with passion and honesty about his adopted home of 45 years, and in this modest volume manages to provide more context and insight than history books three times at fat.

3. *Thai Hawker Food* by **K.Yee, C.Gordon & S.Win** (**BPS Publications, B195**) is possibly this city's most underrated book. It provides illuminating explanations on practically every type of street food in Bangkok, accompanied by entertaining illustrations, cultural anecdotes, maps of top hawker food sites around the city and a glossary of dishes and related terms. An essential urban manual for foodies.

4. *Bangkok People* by **James Eckhardt** (**Asiabooks, B425**) is a good read for anyone interested in some of the more colorful personalities that comprise Bangkok's peculiar human mosaic. Eckhardt profiles a diverse range of Bangkokians, from business tycoons and kick boxers to slum-dwellers, socialites and singers.

5. *Lonely Planet Bangkok* (**Lonely Planet, B850**) is a precious tool for travelers aiming to get the most out of their stay in the capital. The book's excellent language and food sections remind us why author Joe Cummings is still considered the leading Thailand travel guru. This latest (2005) edition underwent a refreshing facelift, including a cleaner layout, better maps and easier navigation.

6. *A Walking Tour in Bangkok* by **architect G.Byrne Bracken** (**Time Editions, B395**) suggests interesting walks through the city's shophouses, temples and markets, accompanied by a dozen useful maps and over 80 fine illustrations.

7. *Insight Guides: Bangkok* (**Insight/Discovery Channel, B750**) looks like one of those clichéd, brochure-style guidebooks, but in fact is loaded with useful information and thoughtful takes on the city, interesting social and cultural features, good historical background and solid photography.

8. *What Can We Do Today – Kids in Bangkok* by **Sue Adams** (**B350**) is a laminated card deck comprising 52 creative ideas for things to do & see with children in Bangkok. Great for those weekends when the kids are driving you nuts and you can't recall the name of that damned water park.

9. *Farang* (**B100**) is a refreshingly independent (and frequently deranged) monthly magazine aimed primarily at the Khaosan Road backpacker crowd. It covers not just Bangkok but other parts of Thailand, Laos, Cambodia, and beyond. *Farang's* insightful features and useful info pages make it a good tool for anyone interested in regional travel, local culture and Bangkok nightlife.

ACKNOWLEDGEMENTS

Our greatest debt is to our publisher, Mark Hanusz, who in the course of this frenzied project tolerated endless delays and excessive nonsense. Mark threw his weight behind this book from the very start and kept it there throughout, guiding us wisely with a 'hard love' mix of encouragement and discipline. He has officially graduated: After working with us, he can presumably put up with anyone.

Sasa Kralj – friend, teacher, and Sufi juggler extraordinaire – injected heart and soul into this volume with wonderful images and unique insights from the streets of Bangkok. This is his book as much as it is ours.

Sung Thanutvorn Jaturongkavanich – leading researcher, content reviewer, in-house critic and wonderful friend – worked overtime to provide critical, no-nonsense insights on every chapter, making this book a far better product.

Thanks also to David Pottebaum for regular encouragement, thoughtful feedback and numerous insights; to John Hanusz for his careful editing and proofreading; to Martin Cejie for the funky cover shot; and to Paul Dillon for the thorough round of last-minute editing.

Our gratitude also to Dr. Chalinee Hirano; Potjanee Chatchaiwiwattana; Ann Suchawadee Jarak; Tanes Petsuwan and Vunsadej Thavarasukha at TAT; Suli Widodowati and Miranthi C. Dewi at Equinox; Jerome Ming; Hasief Ardiasyah for helping on edits; Tom van Blarcom at TQPR Thailand; Majestic Suites Resort Hua Hin; Phornphirun Place; Clarissa Meister-Petersen; Shari Kessler; Josh Estey; Yvan Cohen at Asiaworks Photos; Marc Laban and Heather Kelly from Asiaworks; Kavi Chongkittavorn at the *Nation*; Asiabooks; Jentana & Associates; Yokee Playboy; Philip Cornwel-Smith; Crazy driver of bus No.71 (green); Crazy conductor of bus No.71 (green); Ian Mader; Palani Mohan; Somporn Panyastianpong; Songchai Ratanasuban; Chris Brummitt; Simon Montlake; Daniel Cooney; Kathleen Reen; Uri Tadmor; Cosme René Carbonell Pulido; Modern Dog; Lawan Jirasuradej; Yvan Van Outrive.

GUY WISHES TO THANK: Shlomo, Rina, Smadar, Michal and Tsivi Sharett for their love and support across three time zones; Arif Hasyim; Nancy-Amelia Collins; Ping Amranand; Ou Baholyodhin; Raul Carbonell Pulido; Vinai Dithajohn; Ran Ezer; Jennifer Gampell; Jeanne Hallacy; Daniel Kestenholz; Man with umbrella; Sigal & David Regev; Phiset Saat-Yen; Angela Takats; Frank Chairat Thomya; Michael Töpffer; Asaf Weinberger; Francis Wittenberger; Apichaya Wuttipongpreecha; Ami Zarchi.

DANIEL WISHES TO THANK: Vishalini Lawrence for her enthusiasm, unwavering support and constant encouragement; Josh Kreger, for all the usual crap; Boyd Kosiyabong; Jenny Geib; all my great friends in Jakarta who made fun of me for thanking them last time; Yindee Lertcharoenchok; Marcus Mietzner; Farah 'Fairy' Madhzan; Linda & Zeish & Nomi; Elana & Claudio & Ombù Maurice Ance (welcome from the inside out!); my dearest Savta; and the warm, wonderful three-ring circus that is the Feldstein, Creemer and Eichler clans.

PHOTOGRAPHY

All photographs by Sasa Kralj except:

Page **10** Karaoke Teen (Daniel Ziv); **16-17** Beauty Pageants (The Nation); **24-27** Chatuchak (Daniel Ziv); **28-29** Chic (Daniel Ziv); **32-33** Comics (Jerome Ming); **34-35** DIY Dining (Jerome Ming); **40-41** Fakes (Daniel Ziv); **56-57** Hi-So/Lo-So (Daniel Ziv); **64-65** Kathoey (Daniel Ziv); **78-79** Lottery (Jerome Ming); **88-89** MBK (Daniel Ziv); **92-93** Mobile Phones (Daniel Ziv); **102-105** Nana (Daniel Ziv); **110-111** Pharmacies (Daniel Ziv); **112-113** Phra Athit (Jerome Ming); **118-119** Retro (Poster - Guy Sharett Private Collection); **122-123** 7-Eleven (Daniel Ziv); **126-127** Sky Train (Jerome Ming); **136-137** Tabloids (Guy Sharett); **144-145** Touts & Gem Scams (Jerome Ming); **164-171** Grace Hotel Photos (Daniel Ziv).

SASA KRALJ is a Croatia-born photojournalist who abandoned life as a marketing manager in Zagreb to document war, spirituality, and urban culture in the Balkans, Southern Africa, Indonesia, Thailand, Bangladesh, Egypt and Iraq. His photos have appeared in the *New York Times*, *Newsweek*, *The Guardian*, *Business Week*, *Far Eastern Economic Review* and numerous other publications in Asia and Africa. He established the photography department at *Djakarta!* magazine, and has led workshops for young photographers in Cape Town, Jakarta and Dhaka.

other titles from Equinox Publishing